HOPDANCE

HOPDANCE

STEWART PARKER

Edited by **MARILYNN RICHTARIK**
Foreword by **LYNNE PARKER**

THE LILLIPUT PRESS
DUBLIN

First published 2017 by
THE LILLIPUT PRESS
62–63 Sitric Road, Arbour Hill
Dublin 7, Ireland
www.lilliputpress.ie

ISBN 978 1 84351 709 2

A CIP record for this title is available from
The British Library.

10 9 8 7 6 5 4 3 2 1

Set in 11.5 pt on 15 pt Centaur by Marsha Swan
Printed in Spain by GraphyCems

Contents

Foreword

In 1961 Stewart, my uncle, won his first battle with the vengeful disease that would eventually take his life at the height of his creative powers. Having encountered death while still a teenager he found within himself the resources to live, joyously, in the full awareness of the 'wave as tall as a ship . . . creeping soundlessly towards him over the dark water'.

The diagnosis of bone cancer, and the amputation that followed it, happened a few months after I was born. I knew him only in his post-operative state; yet as a small child I had almost no awareness of his physical disability, apart from once glimpsing a prosthetic limb on the stairwell of my grandparents' house. I was curious, but being as solipsistic as most three year-olds I must have placed the image in a drawer somewhere in my head, and promptly closed it.

In 1964 Stewart left Belfast to take up a university teaching post in America, so our real acquaintance only began in earnest when he returned in 1969. For my sister Julie and me he was chiefly associated with Christmas; a magical, somewhat exotic figure, replete with the stylishness of 1960s New York State bohemia, adding saturnalian spice to a jovial but very ordinary family party. Thrillingly, he would write a short play for us to perform for the rest of the family on Boxing Day. Later, as a fledgling theatre director, I would grow to know him in much greater depth, and have been able to direct his plays throughout my career; his influence on my own work has been profound.

Apart from his very distinctive gait, the image I hold of Stewart is one of warmth, fun, festivity, colour – life. There was never a sense of disability.

Reading this novel now brings me to another image entirely, one apparently at odds with the first, but an essential part of his identity. It brought home to me the effect on my family, their helpless, dogged visits to the hospital, the reference to 'his brother's unarticulated anguish' expressed in the gift of a radio.

After the visceral shock of the diagnosis, the amputation and the – almost more devastating – terror of a recurrence in the other limb, you begin to appreciate the expansive vision that allows him to absorb his trauma and ultimately turn it to use. The intellectually muscular, playfully confident dramatist of *Spokesong* in 1975, harnessing history to music hall turns, is also the 'spectral stranger in the corner' that he describes seeing his amputated figure in the mirror for the first time. His illness and treatment connect him equally to the brute reality of the physical world, and to the netherworld of hospitalization and hallucinogenic pain relief; as he observed, his writing draws on 'multiplying dualities'. *Hopdance* focuses clear-sighted, analytical objectivity onto the profoundly vulnerable state of its protagonist. His experience with cancer and amputation did not create this aspect of his personality, but it surely honed its application in his work; and prepared him psychologically to deal with the fragility of his temporal existence.

From childhood Stewart was no stranger to doctors and the rigours of medical treatment. He mischievously parodies their language in his first play, *Spokesong*, imagining Belfast as 'a giant body … diagnosis not good'. That playful reference finds its dark counterpoint in the last great speech of *Northern Star*, when the city has become 'as maddening and tiresome as any other pain-obsessed cripple'.

The close call with death was to permeate much of his work — the most vivid and direct treatment taking shape in *Nightshade*, his play about an undertaker who is also a magician, and who is thus practising two forms of illusion. This play, which contains some of his most beautiful dramatic prose, echoes *Hopdance*; in its connections to Shakespeare and to the biblical story of Jacob, but in particular to the Fair Rosa legend, the tale of the Sleeping Beauty.

A crucial part of its fabric is the gallows humour so bitingly evident in *Hopdance* — the acid, sardonic wit that Tosh harnesses to control his rage and desolation. Dark comedy is the engine of Stewart's work, and his weapon against the deadly parasites of piety and sentiment. 'First he cripples you. Then he gives you his blessing,' says Delia, the Magician's daughter. Later she speaks of death, and our inability to deal with it, as 'an action we perform throughout our lives. And so — at the heart's core — we are the tribe that has lost the knowledge of how to live.'

The origin of that quest for life and the manner of living — voiced by Delia in *Nightshade*, articulated and resolved by Marian in his last, majestic play *Pentecost* — can be traced to *Hopdance*. This vibrant novel demonstrates the humour and intellectual discipline that enabled Stewart to transcend the death of a part of himself. He went on to achieve a monumental body of work that expressed fully his personality, philosophy and vision. He was the least crippled person I've ever known.

My thanks, and those of my family, to Marilynn Richtarik, who has worked tirelessly to capture the complexity of an extraordinary writer. *Hopdance*, which she has edited with such precision and judgment, gives further invaluable insights in addition to those contained in her perceptive biography. Thanks also to Antony Farrell and Lilliput for this splendid publication.

Lynne Parker, Dublin

Note on the Text

At age nineteen, during his second year as a student at Queen's University Belfast, Stewart Parker learned that he had Ewing's Tumour, a rare form of bone cancer. The only effective treatment for it then entailed removal of the diseased limb before the cancer could spread, and so, on 17 May 1961, surgeons at the Royal Victoria Hospital in Belfast amputated his left leg above the knee. Parker remained in hospital for three months, then spent the rest of the summer convalescing at home before returning to university that fall. Desiring fervently at the time to appear merely inconvenienced by his loss, he threw himself back into his old activities with an intensity that left him little opportunity to reflect on it.* For nearly a decade following his ordeal, however, Parker lived with the uncomfortable knowledge that the cancer could recur. Only when this apprehension had begun to fade could he admit to himself what a heavy burden he had been carrying since his diagnosis, and he decided to attempt to capture in writing the period before, during, and immediately after his hospitalization. As he confided to an interviewer in 1977,

---

* For an account of Stewart Parker's cancer diagnosis, treatment, and gradual recovery, see chapter three of my biography of him, published by Oxford University Press in 2012.

he sought to exorcise the trauma by getting it out of his head and onto the page.* (His protagonist, Tosh, defines the 'artistic impulse' as 'the obsessive need to rehearse your memory of hell': 'If you don't enact it from time to time, it'll rend out your heart.') Conversely, he may have wanted to preserve his memories of that phase of his life before they lost their sharp edges. Most of all, though, recording the experience allowed him to structure it for himself in such a way as to endow it with meaning.

In early 1970, Parker began planning a screenplay about his amputation, and he eventually started writing it in January 1971. Likely stymied by the intractably psychological nature of what he wished to convey, however, he never completed more than a few scenes of this. By January 1972, when he returned to the subject, he had probably decided to write his story as a novel instead, although he kept the same title for it: *Caution In the Traffic, Prudence In the Rain*. (He would not rename it *Hopdance* until 1974.) Parker finally achieved some momentum on the work early in 1972 after assigning himself a daily quota of 300 words, a tactic intended to help him make headway on his most artistically ambitious projects even amid the pressures of paid work with urgent deadlines. This method of composition, together with the text's genesis as a screenplay, likely influenced its structure of short, vivid vignettes. He worked on the novel through 1972 and 1973, completing a draft of it in September 1973. Within a week, though, he began tinkering with the order of the sections. From the beginning, he had conceived of the work's structure as non-chronological – inserting, for example, scenes from before Tosh's cancer diagnosis between scenes taking place after it – but now he exchanged one non-chronological arrangement for another one, in some cases cutting handwritten scenes apart with scissors and taping them back together in a different order.

---

* Caroline Walsh, 'Stewart Parker', *The Irish Times*, 13 August 1977.

Parker began typing what he then regarded as the 'final draft' of the novel in October 1973, but managed only a few sections before losing the impetus to continue. In January 1975, having already reached the decision to focus in future on drama, he returned to *Hopdance* once again and started typing it from the beginning. 'Can't make up my mind', he remarked in his journal:

> I've spent too long considering it, I don't know what it's trying to be anymore. Only thing that's certain is, it's too short for publishers. Am apathetic about it for over a year now. Oh, well. Finish and be damned. There are certainly good phrases in it, here and there. Treat it as a daily chore, be done in a couple of months. Thereafter concentrate on plays, I think now my major energy shd. be applied there.

This time, the effort to produce a typescript foundered before the bottom of the ninth page.

Had Parker considered *Hopdance* to be a commercial proposition, which he clearly did not, he might have managed to finish it at this juncture. In the absence of any financial incentive, though, he felt more enthusiasm about his first full-length stage play, *Spokesong*, in development at the time. In truth, as he remarked later, the novel's writing had been propelled by an overwhelming psychological need. Once he had drafted the scenes, however, the sense of urgency deserted him. He put away the manuscript, satisfied that it had served a 'therapeutic purpose' for him.*

Although his work life now revolved around play-writing, Parker never forgot about his autobiographical novel, and, at times both of unusual stress and of unaccustomed time for contemplation, his thoughts reverted to it. In late February 1982 ('On an impulse,' as he noted in his journal), he 're-read passages of *Hopdance*, & made notes towards completing it. Must do. Somehow. This year.' Sporadically, over the ensuing months, Parker worked on the novel, making

---

* Walsh, 'Stewart Parker.'

minute changes to the existing manuscript and playing yet again with the order of the scenes. This was the year in which Parker's marriage, troubled for some time, broke down entirely – partly as a result of his falling in love with someone other than his wife. He was, simultaneously, undergoing a crisis of confidence in himself and his work. He had both the urge and the opportunity to revisit *Hopdance*, but he lacked the tranquillity necessary to focus on it. By the time he regained his emotional equilibrium the following year, he had entered a particularly frenetic phase of his career as a dramatist that did not abate until the last months of 1987.

In the summer of 1988, Parker returned at last to his novel. He had decided to add several new scenes to it, and he drafted three of these between July and October: Tosh's conversation with his tutor, Larmour, about Thomas Rhymer; a debate between Tosh and another student about the relative value of literature and political action; and a scene in which Tosh gives a presentation to a group of schoolboys. He also wrote out yet another plan for *Hopdance* and seemed determined to rework the book from beginning to end. The most recent additions to the manuscript consist of ten word-processed pages representing the first six scenes of the projected final version. In a sadly ironic twist, however, a diagnosis of terminal stomach cancer in September derailed Parker's progress. Initially told that, with treatment, he might live for another year, he tried frantically to keep working on *Hopdance*, but, in the event, he died on 2 November 1988, leaving the novel unfinished.

Hopdance has fascinated me since June 1994, when Parker's executor, Lesley Bruce, allowed me to examine it. I knew the novel had never achieved the apotheosis Parker had envisaged for it, but to my mind it possessed a raw power even in its patchwork state. Although incomplete in Parker's terms, its form meant that there were no obvious holes or gaps in it. Fragmentary by nature, it readily accommodated new fragments – and could just as easily do without them. It therefore seemed possible to me to produce an edited version of *Hopdance* that, while not fulfilling Parker's ultimate vision for it, at least would not do violence to it.

As a writer of experimental prose, Parker wished to challenge novelistic conventions regarding linear structure and character development by illustrating, as he had explained in notes towards an earlier unpublished novel, *The Jest-Book of ST Toile*, 'simultaneity of event and stasis of character... pitted against an alarmingly unpredictable universe.' Since, he had argued then, 'life is largely lived, not in the present tense, but in the continuous past tense,' he rejected the idea of 'a step-by-step narrative' in favour of 'a sequence of narrative images which will enact themselves simultaneously in the reader's mind when he has finished reading them by the intricate way in which they are connected.' As Parker's alter ego, Tosh, explains to his friend Harrison in *Hopdance*, 'You take the fragments of your past... You fit them into whatever mosaic seems to work. It has nothing to do with time or space' – except that, in his own case, 'figments' might be a more appropriate description of them: 'I remember single incidents with surrealistic intensity, they never happened the way they replay themselves in my head. Most of them were insignificant at the time. I've forgotten all the big production numbers. But these small moments obsess me.'

The non-chronological aspect of the novel apparently became less important to Parker over the course of composition; in successive revisions he often took pains to clarify the time frame of the scenes that depart from chronology through the addition of signposting words such as 'had'. Nevertheless, the episodes retain the sense of being suspended in time rather than definitively linked in it. Each section of *Hopdance* has a coherence of its own, but each also gains from association with the others both before and after it, so that individual incidents gain resonance on repeated readings of the book.

The sections of *Hopdance* that Parker drafted last — as well as those he wanted, but was not able, to write at the end of his life — were designed to make more overt a theme implicit in the version of the novel he completed in 1973. Tosh is adrift before his cancer diagnosis, plagued by the twin 'cankers' of a puzzling pain in his leg and a crippling loneliness. As the story of the amputation and its aftermath unfolds, he begins to allow other people to share his suffering and moves closer to being able to make the great connection he has sought to another human being, although most of the time his efforts are misdirected. Like James Joyce does in *A Portrait of the Artist as a Young Man*, a seminal influence, Parker punctuates Tosh's process of maturation as a person (notably incomplete by the end of the novel) with his reflections on writing. The amputation, Parker suggests, prepares him to become a serious writer by forcing him into a more authentic relationship to life, which even before his surgery Tosh believes 'Starts with the wound. Ends with the kiss. For the lucky ones.' (In a late note about *Hopdance*, Parker observed that 'The daemon lover who comes riding over the fernie brae for him is pain.')

The scenes that Parker wrote or intended to write in the 1980s (labelled, on his final plan for the novel, 'He was a student of literature at that time', 'Fat student on the picket line', 'Anybody know 'Fair Rosa'?', 'Country student, Mullan', 'Larmour & Brendan', 'Minister & Jacob', 'The care of posterity is greatest', and 'Larmour and the sacred texts'), together with an existing section on Tosh's proposal for a play about the Ancient Mariner ('Tosh hadn't helped his case'), would have allowed him to illustrate Tosh's developing aesthetic philosophy through analyses of his own 'sacred texts', which he described in notes for the novel as 'Five versions of Sancgreal'. Parker listed and explicated these in another brief note for *Hopdance*:

Jacob the lame.	My condition.
Thomas the rhymer.	My calling.
Rosa the fair.	My poetic soul.

Brendan the Navigator.   My aspiration.
The Mariner.   My fate.

References to these narratives – the biblical account of Jacob, the Scots Border ballad 'Thomas Rhymer', the story commonly known as 'Sleeping Beauty', the legend of St Brendan the Navigator as recounted in the medieval Latin poem *Navigatio Sancti Brendani Abbatis*, and Samuel Taylor Coleridge's 'The Rime of the Ancient Mariner' – crop up repeatedly in Parker's other writings, most obviously in his plays *Nightshade* and *Pratt's Fall*, and they were charged for him with deeply personal significance. The overall effect of including extended meditations on them in *Hopdance* would have been to make the novel more self-reflexively about the creation of art and his own initiation into its mysteries. Notes towards the 'Country student' scene indicate that Parker even intended to foreshadow his protagonist's future vocation as a playwright by having him realize that drama could offer a way of reconciling his contradictory impulses 'to make a proclamation of my own uniqueness' and 'to lose every vestige of signature'.

These late additions to *Hopdance* would not, however, in my opinion, have significantly changed Parker's conception of the scenes he had written in the early 1970s. As a rule, he composed slowly and carefully, and the initial handwritten drafts of his works are remarkable for their tidiness. He generally preferred sitting for half an hour without writing a line to forcing himself to set words down that he knew from the outset would only have to be rewritten, if not rethought. When he typed a work he usually revised it, clarifying themes and polishing diction and syntax without fundamentally altering the substance of it. This general predilection was likely intensified in the case of *Hopdance*, the episodes of which he contemplated for years before ever putting pen to paper. The manuscript bears traces of Parker's repeated returns to it, but he rarely changed more than a word or phrase here and there on the pages dating from the 1970s. He would certainly have introduced further changes at the typing stage, but I think it unlikely that the final versions of existing sections would have differed dramatically from the original ones. The context of such scenes would be altered by the addition of new ones, but they would keep their initial significance within the story of the amputation while gaining new meanings in the expanded narrative of Tosh's artistic development.

It thus seemed feasible to me to try to prepare a publishable version of the novel based on the manuscript as it existed at the time of Parker's death. The first decision I made as editor was to include all the scenes that Parker had drafted, in the order in which they appear on his final plan for *Hopdance*, although I recognize that the resulting version falls between the one he completed in the 1970s and the one he envisaged in 1988. This struck me as a pragmatic way of honouring Parker's intentions for the work while acknowledging the limits of my own knowledge and understanding of them.

I address some of these limitations in my appendices to the novel itself. The first three deal with the ordering of the scenes, a subject of great importance to Parker himself. Although non-chronological, the arrangement of the sections was hardly arbitrary. Parker thought about this throughout the process of composition and reconsidered it on several occasions. I have to confess, however, that I do not know why he regarded one ordering as better than another. In the hope that others might be able to infer the logic behind Parker's rearrangements of the vignettes, I have included his successive plans for the novel in appendices 1 through 3.

Appendix 4 concerns a section labelled 'The care of posterity is greatest' on Parker's final plan. The title matches the epigraph of an essay he wrote on the fifth anniversary of his amputation in 1966 and rediscovered in his study in 1979. This essay is inserted into the *Hopdance* manuscript, along with another prose piece from 1966 and a much shorter fragment probably written in the 1980s, after the section in the novel that describes Tosh writing an essay on 'the state of poetry in contemporary society' just before his amputation. Parker probably intended this section to represent Tosh's essay, but it is not clear how or if the 1966 pieces would have featured in it. It was, however, apparent to me that the narrative ground to a halt at this point if the 1966 essays and the later fragment were read in their entirety here, so I took the decision to include them all with an explanatory note in an appendix, rather than leaving them in their original forms in the text itself.

Parker wrote *Hopdance* over a period spanning nearly two decades, during which he lived in both the UK and the US, and, unsurprisingly, the manuscript displays inconsistencies. My work on this edition of the novel began with transcribing what Parker had written as precisely as I could, followed by an effort to standardize accidentals in as unobtrusive a way as possible. Early on, I decided to correct Parker's spelling where necessary, using the *Oxford English Dictionary* as my authority, although I preserved Parker's preference for 's' over 'z' in words that could take either. On the other hand, I chose to leave his eccentric punctuation largely alone, knowing that Parker cared deeply about the rhythm of his words and sentences. Occasionally, however, I added full stops at the end of sequences not experimental in form when I judged their omission to be an oversight on his part. After a period of agonized indecision, I decided to treat hyphenation as an issue of spelling rather than of punctuation. I have standardized compounds, which Parker treated very inconsistently indeed, according to the usage in the *Oxford English Dictionary*. Where the OED gave more than one spelling in bold at the beginning of an entry, I chose the one Parker had used if it were an option. In cases where a compound employed by Parker was not included in the OED, I left it as he had written it.

At the end of his life Parker typed out on a computer the first six scenes of the novel (including both new and old ones), and this word-processed segment provided a template for the layout of the whole.

It is, for example, clearer in this word-processed segment than it is on the manuscript pages that Parker typically began paragraphs with a normal indentation. (In the early 1970s, the impecunious young author wrote like someone who did not know where his next pad of paper would come from, with little in the way of margins, so in the manuscript it is often easier to tell where a paragraph ends than where one begins.) I have generally preserved Parker's idiosyncratic punctuation, including his frequent omission of question-marks, substitution of commas for full stops, and use, following Joyce's example, of dashes instead of quotation-marks.

Where Parker underlined words in the manuscript, I have italicized them. I have also italicized block quotations, for clarity, and begun each paragraph apart from the first in each section with a normal indentation. I have standardized Parker's use of dashes when conversational tags or descriptive passages intervene between parts of a speech by a single character, adding a second dash in cases where the interruption consists of more than a few words, and standardized capitalization in a couple of scenes where Parker's treatment of it varied (the Mariner, the Professor). I have inserted two blank lines between sections of the novel labelled separately on his final plan for it and one blank line to mark breaks within sections.

Throughout the editorial process, my aim has been to present, to the best of my ability, Parker's words, while minimizing the distraction presented by stylistic inconsistencies. I want the reader's experience of *Hopdance* to be that of encountering a new novel by a contemporary writer, so I have avoided drawing attention to my procedures in the text itself, confining such comments to this note and the appendices. I am tremendously grateful to Lesley Bruce and Parker's estate for allowing me to undertake this labour of love and giving me a free hand in its completion, and to Antony Farrell and The Lilliput Press for making the book available to a general readership. I would also like to acknowledge the invaluable assistance provided by Mary Grace Elliott, who painstakingly helped me to check the typescript through several drafts and to formulate the rules by which the work would be carried on, and by Tom McHaney, Bernard MacLaverty, Glenn Patterson, Parker's agent Alexandra Cann, and my agent Jonathan Williams. I thank Georgia State University's Department of English, Queen's University Belfast, the US–UK Fulbright Commission, and the Hambidge Center for Creative Arts and Sciences for funding, time, and space with which to pursue the project, and, as always, I am thankful to Matt, Walker, and Declan Bolch for sharing the journey with me.

HOPDANCE

The foul fiend haunts poor Tom in the voice of a nightingale.
Hopdance cries in Tom's belly for two white herring.
Croak not, black angel; I have no food for thee.

PART ONE

One day they said, It's time you went to the gymnasium, Mr. Tosh. And so you go there, whistling even, a shanty of sorts. Trying to fancy yourself aboard ship along these long corridors with the curvy low ceilings, a male nurse in his white smock smiling past like a cabin steward. Polished floor, the right crutch sliding a little. Easy. On a real ship, on these things, with one bound you'd be on your arse. All at sea. There now, wordplay even. Of a sort. The boy is back in his mind again.

Tunnelling left, that must be the place, swing-doors with port-holes. Eases his right shoulder between the doors, bundling through in an awkward scuffle, the hospital gymnasium. Bars, ropes, curious engines. Nobody here yet. Heeling round to starboard...

a spectral stranger in the corner lurking there eyeing you out of a ragged thicket of dirty fair hair, lank blue jumper hanging limp on the bony shoulders, metal crutches clamping the forearms, fixing you with that glittering eye, transfixed, don't look down... gross blue knot dangling in the vacant space where the left leg should be, pyjama knot, dangling from the blunt stump fat with its bandages, the one fat thing, gorged full on its own blood. First sight of it. First mirror.

Easy. As others see me. Scary ghost. Sad freak. No wonder they tried to make you wear their long tartan dressing-gown, get a haircut, stay in the ward, spare the feelings of the healthy, no wonder, horrified eyes sliding sideways as they pass me in the corridor.

Motionless, holding the stare. For the slightest move, confirmed by the mirror, will force him at length to identify with that halt scarecrow which now at last stands there revealed to him after the months of living wholly inside that stricken mask. Caught.

Look.

A student of literature at the time, and full of certainties at first. To be nineteen in a warm room, surrounded by books and friendship – the certainties came easy. Outside the window, beyond the great chestnuts and the cultivated lawns, the province yawned along rank and stultifying. On Sundays he could hear the hounds of heaven in the park, a tinny evangelical baying and barking and the whine of hymns, drifting across the damp grey air into his back yard and through the big window to where he stretched across Prudence's tense body for another bottle of Monk from under the bed. The province was without form and void. Darkness moved upon the face of the waters.

He respected Larmour, his tutor, more than the other lecturers in the Department, though warily and grudgingly, for they agreed on virtually nothing.

—You don't find the study of literature a sufficiently rigorous discipline in itself, Mr. Tosh, without shouldering an additional responsibility for creating it?

The voice was a kind of genial sneer, Larmour perched well back in his swivel chair, knees hugged to chest with glee, perpetual monkey grin, a whiff of satan in the black goatee and the dark, mocking eyes.

—The title of writer is one which I intend to win. Tosh was curt and stolid in these encounters, privately convinced of his due destiny.

—Doubtless so, but might you not usefully begin your quest by thoroughly acquainting yourself with the unbroken traditions of nine centuries of major achievement?

—Tradition is meaningless to me.

—Then you are either a remarkably obtuse young man, since tradition is of course synonymous with meaning, or else a deliberate solipsist, which appears the more likely case whilst being an equally inappropriate position for an honours student in this Department.

Cuddling his knees closer, the sneery grin widening to fill the whole room.

There was a paper to be turned in for each of the three terms, Tosh had elected to write his first one on the Scots Border ballad of *Thomas Rhymer*, provoking Larmour's gleeful scorn.

—You don't consider a solitary ballad rather a meagre subject, Mr. Tosh?

—It's a far from meagre poem.

—It is undoubtedly a fine flower of the oral tradition, but it will scarcely sustain the same degree of detailed scrutiny as a conscious literary artefact.

—That's only one of the things which I admire about it.

—You are not intending to rhapsodise over the beauty of its impersonal voice for the entire three thousand words?

Tosh launching his offensive.

—The ballads are not impersonal. Least of all this one. It's a pre-personal voice. It predates the psychological need for signature. It has no vestige of signature, and yet it has a clear distinctive unmistakable voice, a tone all its own. A point of view. The view of a whole community crystallised into a single voice. It is pre-personal, by the same token that Beckett's work is post-personal.

—That should certainly get us to the bottom of page one, once you have finished defining your terms. What else?

—Thomas lies on Huntley Bank. He spies a woman riding towards him, o'er the fernie brae. A daemon lady. They make love. She takes him on her horse into the Eildon Hills and their other world. If he speaks, she will be sure of his body ever after. My tongue is mine ain, he tells her. She shows him wonders, a river of blood, a forest of bleeding boughs, the roads to heaven, hell and Elfland, she takes him to her castle there. He returns to Ercildoune after thirty days. He has the seer's gift of poetry. He has risked the greatest danger to penetrate the world behind appearances. It's a fable of the creative mystery. The nature of the poet's gift and peril.

—You see yourself in these terms, I take it?

Tosh affixing his stolid frown on the doodles burgeoning across the cover of his Summit Refill Pad Ruled Feint And Margin 80 Leaves Foolscap. A John Dickinson Product.

Everything that day slick or spongy with the rain, dropping down softly and inexhaustibly out of the grey air, so that for a while I failed to notice the tears on her face as we walked the path away from the Union.

—What's the matter, Prudence?

Shaking her head, averting it.

—What are you crying for?

A few sobs bit back, quivering lips contorting her little face in a struggle to speak. Tosh felt the familiar prickle of stifled rage, at her helplessness, Chrissake just spit it out, will you, anything.

—It's just... just... it's the rain, she said, almost gagging on the words.

They walked on through to the main quadrangle.

—We'll sit down, said Tosh.

The wooden seat brimmed with raindrops which glistened into thick wet smears when he brushed at it with his handkerchief. They sat together beneath the black umbrella.

—You don't seem all that keen. Not anymore, she said.

—My leg's sore again today.

—Same place? She gently clasped the front of his knee and rubbed it. Her eyes were dry now.

—I was wondering, she said. What you thought. About getting summer jobs together.

—I feel total lassitude. Soaked right through in it. All the time now. My leg feels kind of hollow inside.

—Is this helping it?

Her hand made an even rustle against the knee of his trousers. The rain murmured down, drips falling off the dark red brick in a multitude of rhythms.

—You still haven't said. She spoke carefully. Whether we're breaking it off. Or what.

—I suppose we are, Prudence.

He held his breath.

—You seem to be losing interest, I know that much.

—Your ears move up and down when you're talking, did you know that?

—You just won't ever be serious about it.

—There's a sort of gentle twitching under your hair, like two field mice. Oh, God.

—You ought to see a doctor about that leg.

The consulate flags hung limp in the rain, as if shamed by the moral force of their frail protest. You were given a placard to carry, reading Make Babies Not Freakshows, and you felt foolish. As though you had any acquaintance with babies, as though a sodden handful of students outside the US consulate-general, in a dwarfish and absurd province, was likely to fend off nuclear armageddon, was not in itself a sad little freak show. Falshaw, student journalist, fat and pustular, confronts you with his round red comedian face, on the picket line.

—How's the daemon lover, then?

—Depends. Is it some daemon who loves me, or me who's supposed to love some daemon?

—Both in your case, I'd say.

—How about the revolution?

—Delayed for the time being, on account of industrial action, listen, you haven't joined the Labour Club yet, people are beginning to talk.

—I prefer writing to joining.

—What you are, Toshy, is what I call a gut socialist. You feel it deep down but you don't think it through, that's okay, we need your type in the movement too.

—I may have a couple of instincts that I'm prepared to credit. I'm not prepared to institutionalise them, though, not quite yet.

—Bourgeois individualism very big danger, artistic types much prone to it. Beware.

A gnarled and greasy man, his eyes balefully magnified by slab-like glasses, passed by on a circuit of his own, counter-clockwise to theirs, clad in a sandwich-board proclaiming Christ Said, Ye Must Be Born Again.

—Christ was the first socialist, you know, Falshaw told the man as he passed.

—I don't accept that, said Tosh. Socialism wasn't founded by Christ at all. It was built on the same rock as Catholicism. Peter the Betrayer. The moment when the cock crew thrice, that was when the party was born.

—Very elegant, said Falshaw. So you imagine you can change the world for the better all on your own? As Jesus S. Tosh?

—If I could even change myself for the better, I'd settle for that.

—So what are you doing marching in my picket?

—If I have to die, I'd sooner die foolish but at least in the right. Instead of foolish and also wrong.

—You are wrong. You're a romantic egotist.

—I'm an agnostic, I'm prepared to wait, till the third time comes round again, for the cock to crow. Then let's see who jumps.

*

—Anybody know 'Fair Rosa'?

Perching on the edge of the classroom desk, tuning the guitar.

—Do Elvis, sir! Sudden chattering laughter of raw boys. Yourself eight years ago, a mere eight. Their oversized knees and ears, the blazers either baggy or starveling, the faint sour odour of their imprisoned force.

—I want you to listen to the story of this, now.

E-Major chord. And in.

> *Fair Rosa was a lovely child*
> *A lovely child a lovely child*
> *Fair Rosa was a lovely child*
> *A long time ago...*

Those who can't, teach. But I suppose it might be forced on me, after graduation, for a year or two at any rate, pending fame. But at any rate a visit like this, sitting in, for a period or two... it was after all a favour of sorts to his old English teacher, who was a head now, of this shiny school newly built of civic aluminium and glass, sober-suited thin bald radiant invigilator, who had plucked you out of this once, out of the thick of a gaggle of scruffs just like these, and nourished your incoherent dreams... a visit like this would do no harm. Nor much good either.

> *A wicked fairy cast a spell*
> *Cast a spell cast a spell*
> *A wicked fairy cast a spell*
> *A long time ago...*

Fair Rosa. Rosa bella. No rose of swich virtu, O my poetic soul, my poetic bookish bullshit soul, remaindered dictionary of quotations, big reduction my arse, couldn't as much as give it away. A kiss will hardly be enough, to wake you from such fretful slumber. Rape maybe. That might turn the trick.

Fair Rosa slept a hundred years
A hundred years a hundred years
Fair Rosa slept a hundred years
A long time ago...

Dreamless sleep. Coma really, except unageing. Suspended in some spare dimension, beyond speech and touch. Stateless. A stateless soul. Kiss me quick.

A handsome prince came riding by
Riding by riding by
A handsome prince came riding by
A long time ago...

Someday my prince will or ponce at least. Because locked in thrall you most certainly are, and never will be entitled to call yourself writer until your voice breaks out of its inherited drowse and expresses itself fully and freely to the world or at least another, and that is why your efforts to date have been entirely worthy of the name Tosh: well named you are.

He took Fair Rosa by the hand
By the hand by the hand
He took Fair Rosa by the hand
A long time ago...

Abruptly he stopped playing.

—Hands up anybody who's ever heard tell of the Sleeping Beauty story?

One was prepared to admit to it, a silver-haired waif.

—I seen it on TV, sir.

—The Sleeping Beauty is the same story as Fair Rosa. Beautiful princess, cursed by a wicked fairy spell, pricks her thumb on a spindle, is plunged into a dreamless sleep, for a hundred years, she's only eventually wakened because a prince accidentally finds his way through the woods into her castle.

Starts with the wound. Ends with the kiss. For the lucky ones.

He picked on a fat, older-looking boy.

—Suppose you were the prince, what would you do? Would you kiss her?

Puckered lips softly detonating all around the clamorous room. The fat boy unexpectedly blushed.

—I think you'd all be too embarrassed to kiss her.

—Depends what she looks like, sir.

Yelping. Pups delirious for a scent they can't yet smell.

—She looks out of this world, lying there, asleep. It'll take some nerve to wake her. It's a gamble, you might live to regret it, bitterly. You might be waking her up to a life of inconsolable loss. So maybe your nerve fails. Maybe you tiptoe quietly out, climb back up on your horse, and amble home to a quiet, uneventful life. Maybe you should let sleeping beauties lie. If you find one. You do have to decide, though. For the chances are, you'll never ever find your way to the castle a second time.

The roughly sketched faces gazing blindly up, wondering what I'm telling them. As I gaze inscrutably back, wondering what it is I'm telling myself.

On the way out he was joined by a teacher called Redpath, dark baggy shiny suit, creased cream shirt, and the soiled blue university tie with the little crest on it. Together they walked by the school railings, Redpath looking sideways at Tosh's limp, pushing his black-rimmed glasses back on to the bridge of his nose.

—Have you caught a dose of something?

—I doubt it, there's a pain under my knee, that's all.

—Oh aye? Don't fancy the sound of that, they'll probably need to take it off at the bollocks.

Tosh folded his left leg up at the knee and hopped along with great leaps, clinging to the iron railings, leering and squawking,

—Pieces of Eight! Pieces of Eight!

Redpath stood on the kerb uneasily, pushing the glasses up his nose.

—I don't see much likelihood of you becoming a bloody teacher. You're not the sort, if you ask me.

They resumed walking, down towards the school bus-stop twisted drunkenly askew.

Tosh said:

—I don't honestly know what in hell's teeth to do with my life.

—I don't belong in the bloody racket myself, actually, continued Redpath. Most of the time I could laugh in their faces in that staff-room. Bitchy lot of oul hoors, that crowd.

—How do you see yourself, then?

—It's the short hours and three months in the summer, that's what got me into it. The money's pitiful. Still, you need something to keep Mr. Wolf at bay, that's the bugger of it.

—So what do you fancy doing?

—Me? I'm a writer actually.

A funeral came round the corner of the conversation. They observed a short silence.

—What kind of stuff do you write, mostly? asked Tosh.

—Ach, stories. I'm working on a novel, actually.

He fumbled the black-rimmed glasses up his nose in saying this.

—What's it about?

—It's about a teacher.

—You take the fragments of your past, said Tosh. You fit them into whatever mosaic seems to work. It has nothing to do with time or space.

The car bucketed crazily along the twisting roads, Fearn at the wheel, Harrison's girl beside him, Tosh and Harrison in the shadowy back seat.

—That's okay if your mind's impressionistic, said Harrison. Like yours is. Mine's not. I can remember everything. Faces, places, names, the lot. My past is stretched out in detail. I don't remember just fragments.

—It's really figments, with me. I remember single incidents with surrealistic intensity, they never happened the way they replay themselves in my head. Most of them were insignificant at the time, I've forgotten all the big production numbers. But these small moments obsess me sometimes. I'm losing touch with real life.

Fearn told Tosh he should read Jung, and talked about Jung till they drew up at another pub. They drank again and drove on into the growing night, falling silent. Tosh gave himself up to the brusque motions of the car, letting his body shift and roll freely in the choppy sea of Fearn's driving. You're living the life of a somnambulist, there must be more in the world than you can see. Fleeting moments and bits fleeing past, how can you break this paralysis.

They got to the town at three in the morning, the festival had been going on already for three days, they entered it like dream shapes joining a pub crawl. There was a party, Harrison investigated accommodation. They were to sleep in the flat, it was somebody called Henry's, he sat there, soft-voiced drunken bombast, horn-rims, fingers languid in the lank blond hair, the drink all done, he was drinking bathroom cologne. The hall where the one-acts were playing was in a suburb, Tosh walked up a hill, the sun burning him, searching for it. Inside, Harrison wearing his pallid face contorted with surly neurotic tension, they put together a makeshift set, bed borrowed from somewhere, table, detritus from backstage. Tosh could remember nothing about the play they were soon to act, the play they had composed together, improvising scene by scene, he couldn't muster the strength to ask himself questions about it. The bright day faded, they switched on the lights, nobody had arrived, with half an hour to go. Then in drifted ghostly figures, as if casualties of a crash. They were the crew and some of the cast of the three-act entry, hardly able to stand after three days and the performance the previous night and the party all night since it. They slumped onto benches, keeled over asleep on chairs, lay against each other, rested faces in their hunched arms. The adjudicator appeared, the curtain drifted aside, they started, Tosh moved through a calm ballet of pain. Laughter gusted out of odd corners, lights rose and fell, there was a smell of sleep, Harrison's staccato voice and squat jerky figure moved in and out of his line of vision. At the end the loud reports of clapped palms was startling in its sudden eruption. They joined the flopped figures in the dark auditorium for the adjudicator's remarks, he spoke about a new renaissance in the theatre, stirrings of new voices, he picked out a line from the play and repeated it many times; it rattled round the walls like a piece of the play that had broken off. That night they could find nowhere to sleep. They moved around the street, Harrison browbeating festival committee members. They finally lay down on the floor-boards of a loft, with their coats over them. The next day was adjudication, they went drinking and heard applause exhaled like a long rapturous breath from the lighted hall, they heard the three-act entry had won over-all first prize, their own had not won. There was a party that night in a luxury bungalow outside the town, the owner a swaggering loudmouth boasting he would take a guerilla band to fight in the Middle East. A Guinness barrel but no glasses. They queued with milk bottles which filled up with foam. Harrison almost fought with the owner. Tosh sought listlessly amongst the scented crush for a girl to dance and to hold on to, eyes all round devouring each other. He ended up swaying with a plain, gentle girl from

their own crowd. They drove home the next day, Fearn worse at
the wheel than ever, Harrison and Tosh semi-conscious in the back.

—How's your knee? said Harrison when they dropped him off.

—There's a swelling, said Tosh.

Buses and crudely decorated floats were parked all along the kerb to
take the students to different areas of the city. Tosh caught her seeing
him as he jumped on to a bus and up its stairs.

—Shit, he said.

—What's up? asked Harold Gams.

—Nothing. My leg twinged.

—Use your crutch.

Tosh was dressed up as Long John Silver. He had tied the crutch
to his left shoulder, letting it dangle from the armpit, and a stuffed
cockatoo to his right shoulder. His eyepatch was purple and his earrings were curtain rings.

Harold Gams and his crowd were dressed in non-representational
costumes. Harold was wearing a sun-bonnet of his mother's, a pyjama
jacket, a striped rugby jersey with his legs through the arms, a pair of
corsets and climbing boots. He was going to be an accountant and
he had a slight stammer and a nervous abruptness of manner. His
crowd were mainly mountaineering club and fond of healthy pranks.
They liked the Rag but they worked assiduously with their collecting
boxes as well as horsing around.

—There's your little Prudence, said Harold, looking through the
window.

—I saw her. She isn't getting on this bus, is she?

—She's on a float.

—Thank God she's some pride left.

They got off the bus at Government buildings and ran for the
main door shaking their collecting boxes, but police were on duty

to keep them out. From the upper stories, secretaries began throwing down coins to them. They ran round and round the building in a thickening hail of coins. When they had picked all of them up, they ran downhill to another building and charged between the secretaries' desks, collecting what they could before the commissionaires caught up with them and threw them out. After an hour or so of this, they headed for a bus-stop, Tosh using his crutch, exhausted.

—How're you holding out? asked Harold Gams.

—I think I've chafed my armpit. What are you doing after lunch?

—We'll be on the Mountaineering float in the procession. Want to come?

—I was in the procession last year, it was too much like the zoo – watching the crowds watching you. I think I'll freelance with Herb Andrews.

Herb Andrews was a large clumsy lecherous fellow, haplessly unsuccessful at everything he attempted. His plan was for him and Tosh to drive round the city in a Volkswagen chasing girls and catching them, in the cause of charity. As with Harold Gams, Tosh had acceded in a frozen panic for escape.

The first time they screeched to a halt and went whooping after a female figure she turned round and turned out to be a brisk young matron who put coins in their tins and then asked for a lift across the city. As Herb Andrews sheepishly drove Tosh talked to her about the system of one-way streets.

—We've got to handle them more rough, said Herb after this, screeching up alongside a line of girls walking, and leaping into their midst. Tosh got half out on the other side and watched as the girls grabbed hold of Herb and battered him over the head and shoulders with their fists. They had green factory tunics under their coats and most of them had cropped hair and tight mouths. An interested crowd was quickly assembling. At last Herb tore free and managed to get the Volkswagen door closed. They drove out from under the drumming of fists on the roof.

—We'd better only approach them if they're in ones or twos, said Herb, slowing down alongside a single girl who was strolling on the kerb.

—Hop in and we'll take you for a ride, he called to her.

She turned on her heel and walked in the opposite direction. The car crashed into a lamp-post. Herb reversed violently till he was alongside again.

—We'll give you a lift, no kidding, he called. The girl resumed her original direction and the back of the car hit a postbox.

Tosh stopped laughing long enough to say, —For Christ's sake park. We can walk.

As they drove in pursuit of a parking space, he caught sight of a girl with caramel coloured hair and a white fake fur coat walking on the opposite footpath. She walked in free style, almost with an unconscious swagger, swinging a bag on a long strap.

—Stop a minute, he said with sudden urgency.

—We can't park here, pal, said Herb.

—Just stop. Quick.

He already had the door open and was off across the road through the traffic. The girl shrieked when she saw him converging on her, but she made no attempt to run: in fact she stood still. He reached her and put his hands on her shoulders. She had bright eyes and a lively pink mouth.

—Hello, said Tosh. How would you like to have a drink with me this evening?

—Is that your real hair? she said, touching the locks stuck out at odd angles from his pirate's headkerchief.

He kissed her. They kissed each other. He felt a devastating blessed moment of peace. He looked spell-bound with calm into her bright eyes.

—It's for charity, he whispered.

She rested her hands at the nape of his neck. He rested his cheek on the white fake fur arm. They kissed again. He opened his eyes drowsily. She was intently studying his face.

—What's the matter with your leg? she asked.

Then Herb Andrews was lumbering up shouting and whistling, jostling between them, grabbing at the girl, and Tosh was listlessly pushing him and she was running and Herb was following. The enervation flooded him again, redoubled, till he staggered slightly on the way back to the car.

That night he sat with Higgins at closing time, the lights going on and off as the barmen called time.

—I thought you weren't well, said Higgins, conspicuous as the only person in the bar not in costume.

—Certainly I'm not well, said Tosh morosely drunken. I'm dying. I'm dying from the outside towards the middle.

—What are you doing running round as a pirate then?

—I'm such a stupid stupid fucker. She was all set to make a date, I could have been with her right now.

—Jesus, not the furcoat dolly again, you've been moaning about her all night.

The lights went out again, and the barmen cried time as they moved around the tables.

—Listen, said Tosh to the dark hunched form of Higgins. It's all an illusion anyway, it's a con a fantasy a cruel lie.

—What gush are you giving me now?

—I don't know how but they condition us every one to believe it. It's the last thing anybody'll ever give up believing. Nobody wants to give it up, it's their inmost secret, they don't even want to disclose it because it's cherished.

—What? Believe what? What's all this burble about?

—That the answer to whatever ails you is some magic member of the opposite sex, or your own if that's your taste. Some dream lady.

—Your balls, there's nothing like a good ride for a tonic, that's what you need.

—I'm not talking about sex. Sex is the immediate con. I'm talking about love. Love's the ultimate con.

—I could have told you that any time. You're always going morbid and moody about some skinny scrag with a flat chest and big wet eyes. You're not healthy.

—You loved Hazel. Admit it.

Higgins swigged his beer.

—I never did.

—You could have bloody fooled me, in that case. You were as hooked as I've ever been. She can still put the boot in you like nobody else, and if that isn't love — anyway I'm only telling you. Maybe they inject it into you along with the diphtheria and typhoid stuff — the romantic love serum. Maybe they whisper it through your pillow every night when you're asleep — If your leg gets sore, the good fairy in the caramel coloured hair will make it better, all you have to do is buy her a few drinks and invite her to the dance.

—I'm off, said Higgins, rising, Are you going to come to the dance or not?

—I'm going to puke, said Tosh.

The doctor was really his mother's doctor. Tosh had not been in need of a doctor since his schooldays, and the family had been registered in a different surgery then: he had never met this latest man.

Doctors had ruled his mother's life for some years, and at heart she was a revolutionary with regard to them. She passionately desired to overthrow, by force if necessary, their repressive and unjust dictatorship over her body, and to substitute her own rule, diagnosis, treatment and all. But her actions never amounted to more than nervous rebellion, followed by a switch of allegiance to yet another strong-armed healer, more often than not a quack pretender: the family's cards usually travelled with hers. This current doctor was one side of a husband-and-wife team, which was what had won the surgery Tosh's mother's vote. She felt, perhaps, that *in extremis* a power struggle might be initiated and manipulated to her advantage.

The waiting-room was, as in all working-class practices, packed and noisy. An old man's lungs groaned and hirsled in a struggle for more soiled air. A blubber faced baby on the massive knees of his mother sat opposite Tosh staring at him and making a continuous teary sawing sound. One woman told another the detailed, funereal narrative of her gall-stone operation, and then the other described to the one the processes of her daughter's psoriasis, from the first itch, through the dismissal from the bakery job, to the long useless courses of treatment. But the racket could not cover up the yawning pit in the centre of the floor into which they were all staring, the pit common to all waiting-rooms. Whether the inmates are searching for a job or a cure or a loan or a spouse, it is not job cure loan or spouse that they're waiting for. They're waiting to see if they're going to fall into the pit and be swallowed up, or avoid it one more time.

—Now, Mr. Tonk, said the doctor, settling his heavy haunches in the chair without looking up.

—Tosh.

—Tosh, is it, I can never puzzle out that lassie's handwriting.

Loud checked jacket, baggy cavalry twills, the balding head and the whiff of whiskey as he bent over the form. The living cliché of the seedy doctor.

—Oh yes of course, of course, and is your good mother keeping well? Those tablets I prescribed should help her out a good bit. She lets her mind get the better of her, that's the whole trouble. You're at the university isn't that right?

—Right.

—Good man. Any complaints?

Tosh couldn't tell whether this referred to the university or his body. He cleared his throat.

—Did I notice a bit of a limp when you were coming in there?

—Right, that's it.

The doctor pulled a pad towards him with a mechanical abstractedness.

—Where does it pain you?

—Just right here. Under the knee.

—A steady pain, is it?

—Not altogether. It comes and goes. Sometimes it throbs and sometimes the leg just feels hollow.

—Now about how long has it been this way, Mr. Tonk?

Tosh suppressed a smile.

—It's very hard to say. It started very imperceptibly, just sort of crept up on me. But it's over two months, anyway.

—Roll up your trouser leg and let's have a gander.

Tosh pulled the leg of his cords up over his knee. The doctor had red hairy hands with fingers thick as sausages. They moved over the slight vertical swelling under the knee-cap.

—Hmm. Aye. Oh, it's swollen all right.

He turned to the pad and scribbled.

—I'll give you a liniment to rub into it. If it doesn't show any improvement after a few weeks, drop in and see me again. All right, now?

Baldy, Friel, Turf, Singer, Fergy, Deke and Monk: the lads: I can't go on addressing them with these playground names yet here we all are again, hitching lifts again, prodigious drinks again, ostentatious condoms again, Monk's comic, tiny sports car again, Easter weekend in fact again and off to the seaside as at every Easter since puberty turned us all into neurotic wrecks. It can't go on. He looked through the raindrops on Monk's windscreen at the footpaths teeming with youth in heat.

—The Easter charade, he said.

—You're dying to get in there, admit it, said Monk.

—Why the hell did I come? I had no intention of it till you offered the lift last night.

—You're here, have a fling.

—On no money?

—I've no money either, sure. All you need's ingenuity.

—There's Singer and Turf at that corner.

Most of the lads had come down the day before, Thursday, and checked into a hotel room. Singer told them where the hotel was, showing little enthusiasm for Monk's idea of their slipping in and sleeping under the beds. They found the hotel, walked in and up the stairs with a self-consciously non-committal air, and changed in the crowded room. Next door two girls were playing Elvis Presley's *Wooden Heart* on a record player at full volume with the auto changer set to repeat indefinitely. Tosh sat on a bed waiting for Monk, and rested his head against the wall. It was an urban *rite de passage*, this whole outing, and they were too old to be still in need of it. Already the bonhomie was fake. Their frail schoolboy alliance could not withstand the strains of maturity much longer. They would each be dragged irresistibly into the wall niche which society had carved out for them. It was sad.

The fashionable bar this year was a large hotel affair, with long plush wall seats and vast low tables. They drank there and then walked to the ballroom. It sat on rocks facing the sea, a wind was whipping in, hundreds of people were jammed around the ballroom door. Monk had some scheme for getting himself and Tosh in free with somebody else's pass-outs. They swayed and staggered in the crowd, Tosh lost sight of Monk. He searched listlessly and then moved towards the ballroom wall and leaned himself against it, exhausted. The ballroom was obviously full, they weren't letting anybody else in. The wind plucked violently at the shifting crowd. Near Tosh a bunch were horsing around, pulling each other's scarves, singing bits of pop songs, led by a cheerily red-faced girl, clearly a good sport sort of girl. Their silliness was faintly irritating but instead of moving away Tosh exaggerated his posture and rolled his head slowly a few times, with the eyes closed, to indicate suffering.

—Are you all right, fella? The girl was at his side. He opened his eyes a bit but kept them crinkled with pain. She was staring at him inquiringly. Probably a nurse, he thought. No stratagem to sustain the game occurred to him.

—Are you all right? she said again. Tosh nodded stoically and she returned to her cronies.

For the first time in his adult life, he awoke to inconsolable loneliness. It was a kind of heart attack.

While he was lying awake under Turf's bed the next morning, the hotel manager opened the door and entered with the large gesture of a man in authority. Tosh could see only the fawn suedes and the dark grey turn-ups: it was enough.

—I want everybody out of here this minute who hasn't paid the tariff, he announced. It was an oddly pleasant remark: he wasn't evicting the paid-up accessories before the fact, and *tariff* was a pleasing bit of trade jargon, a term that lacked the faintest whiff of lucre. From next door the mechanism of *Wooden Heart* was still grinding on. The manager had all the judicious liberalism of the genuine money-grubber.

—No trouble, no police, he added, as he left.

The lads were in various stages of sleep and toilet. Nobody passed a comment. When Tosh had clothed himself, he and Monk walked out with Deke and Fergy, who also had been freeloading, up the Main Street to the Trocadero Restaurant, and into its gleaming bathroom where they shaved, washed and combed in front of a half-wall of plate glass mirror.

The rest of the day was desultory. They drove around in Monk's car, wandered in and out of amusement arcades, sat over coffee till it was too cold to drink. Every now and then they would run into another lad they knew, often one of a crowd moving along raggedly, and swap noisy jokes. Once it was Higgins. Another time, Tosh was bumped against by a wiry little teenager at the edge of a group, and turned to complain to find the lad crouched down low, ready to fight. Tosh threw himself into an absurd parody of this stance, before realising that the lad was serious. For a moment humour hung in the balance with violence. Then, as though by a signal, everybody resumed their casual dander.

Tosh was puzzled by the degree to which the incident depressed him. He thought through it, and realised that it was because of the vague sense of well-being that had preceded it. But where had that come from? He had not been aware of it till it was brusquely dispelled, but in retrospect it had quite definitely existed; a pervasive sense of harmony, of being well disposed towards the race. He finally traced the source of it to the hotel manager and his tariff.

It was as if his responses had lost all their resilience, had narrowed into a delicate cluster of ganglia which responded sharply to the merest hint of stimulus but was numb to major traumas. O, a sensitive plant.

In the early evening they were back once more in the bar. The meagre money they had arrived with was already gone, so they sponged off Baldy and Singer for a while. Monk had a plan. It entailed waiting till the barmen started calling time. Then they moved around from table to table drinking the abandoned dregs. Some of the dregs were substantial, particularly those left by drinkers in rushing off to vomit. Tosh drank down two full gins, a whiskey and a vodka. The number of available drinks multiplied as the time left in which to drink them shrank. Finally there was nobody left in the bar but Monk and Tosh, dashing around the tables grabbing glasses, pursued by the barmen. By the time they had been slung out in the street, they were successfully drunk.

They rolled on up the street and into a café and over to the first table with two girls sitting at it, a thin one in dark glasses and a plump one wearing a smile. Monk did the required speaking.

—Do you know Julian Ahmed? said the thin girl to Tosh. He's got a smashing Swedish sports car, he's a scream, he's Persian.

Her teeth were very white and even, but not like in a toothpaste commercial; they were human and attractive. Unsmiling, her face was stereotyped in a pallid mould, hardened by the dark glasses.

—I like your teeth, said Tosh.

A cold fog was drifting down the streets. The four of them walked to the guest house in which the girls were sharing a room and went up to the room, but within five minutes they had been evicted by the owner's son. Tosh's drunkenness was turning into a comatose stupidity. He found himself wandering aimlessly through the streets, the thin girl still at his side, still talking. He was aware that he badly needed somewhere warm to sit down. That the only space he had any claim to in the entire town was the passenger seat of Monk's little car. He drifted with the girl to where it was parked and peered down low into its cockpit; it was stuffed full with the bodies of Monk and the plump girl. They walked on. They sat down on a wooden seat wet with the mist, under the bay window of a guest house. The thin girl was still cheerful. He put his arm round her and kissed her, he couldn't understand why she hadn't abandoned him long before, he was such a patently wretched investment. Still she talked, in her dark glasses and pleasant teeth, in the fog that was like the smoke off dry ice, in the damp circles of their buttocks. Her dull warmth comforted the dank chill in his bones. His leg thundered away in a way that made further movement seem unthinkable. Yet he could not stay here and he couldn't just jettison this girl with whom he longed to be wrapped up in a fluffy blanket on a springy bed. He wound himself up for the supreme effort of walking her back to her guest house. When she had gone in, he felt as though there were a slackening in the earth's gravity. He drifted off in a slow and spongy rhythm, every step like a wound stretching and then contracting, every step a beating wound.

It was Turf, the square-faced dependable one, Turf, the stalwart, who found Tosh. Tosh was walking in the dark empty fog, with sightless, unblinking eyes. He showed no signs of recognition when intercepted. He made a few incoherent noises in his throat, like a man checked by grief, but his face was expressionless. He allowed himself to be led to the hotel and put to bed.

At ten o'clock one morning Tosh got up from bed and found that he couldn't walk. In the course of the night his leg had grown entirely brittle. He could no sooner impose his weight on it than on a half-dead branch. He was at his parents' home and had an appointment the following morning with his mother's doctor whose liniment seemed not to have worked. His mother, concerned at his ashen face, helped him into the parental bed whose electric blanket she had switched on. She had to go out, she left him lying staring upwards, his legs suffused in warmth, in the hard grey morning light, in the bedroom heavily overladen with bedside tables and lamps, and dressing table and pouffe and wardrobe and slip rugs and turgid flowers on the wallpaper and candle-wick bedspread.

It must be, he thought. It must be easier if you have the machinery. Machinery of faith. They all have a. There's death, of course, they can walk on into gas chambers smiling. A better life on the far side, what's death? End of the voice in your head, either the end or it goes somewhere else. Anyway it deserts your poor rag doll with its sad knees and armpits. I don't care about life after death, it's a parlour game. The young boy in the. They all have a sort of air of not smugness exactly, but like a successful civil servant. Knowing the system will take care of it all. If you go through the right machinery. All the saved. Is this me, this head voice? Are you Tosh, hey? That warm bath with the wound in its middle down there. That is your body. That's you too. Where does I end? Your shaved off stubble, is that part of this body dragging me down? There, I don't think of it as me, I objectify it. But other times I do, when you come, when you swim. Voice immersed in body. Then I love it. Bodies. I could cry for bodies. If this one's eyes weren't parched. The young boy at the bus-stop. Just looking down on the pity of his thin shoulder-blades, the whole bus irradiated by that. For one moment. A cosmic smile. I could have embraced the world. The astonishing terrible spectacle of us all living our lives. His shoulder-blades were so pathetic. Beatific. Like the Mariner. O my kind heart took pity on me and I blessed them unawares. This body's dragging me away from that. Drowning me. Deep down into my self. Machinery would keep you afloat, if I had any to believe in. Unitive Life. That fulsome jargon: the Mystic Way. I wanted to. I can't abide their sanctimony. Reverential ear-nestness. Repulsive prose. Illumination the Absolute Purgation the Ineffable. Mumbo-jumbo. All I know is. We all crave a fool-proof system. Christ gets institutionalised. Great phoney edifices erected on a couple of insights. A couple of blessed moments long since lost in the giant machinery. Moments isn't enough. We must have a guide to look everything up in. Almanac, star chart. The Word. Oracles to consult. All I know is I'm drowning in my self. I can't believe in any of them. Humanism. Mormonism. Pelmanism. No crutches. No con tricks. Love's the ultimate one. Moments isn't enough. We must have I'll love you until I die. My dream partner. For keeps. O Jesus I. There must be some grounds. O Jesus I can't go on into limbo like this. There must be some ground I can put down feet. Some getting in touch. All these people I know. All these wraiths. They seem to live so remote. I seem to present a different face to each. I don't know one person whole. No person knows me whole. I don't know myself whole. All I know is this foreign body stalled round a swelling. This voice which never shuts up. I may smother. I may smother in my own fabric. I need to rest. I'm too tired.

Tosh woke up that evening and walked downstairs and ate his dinner. The next morning he felt as he had before the collapse. He kept his appointment at the doctor's. The doctor looked at his leg again.

—I tell you what, we'll arrange for a man in the hospital to have a gander at this.

—A specialist, do you mean?

—An orthopaedic man. You sit tight there and I'll give them a tinkle right this minute. While it's fresh in my mind. We might as well settle it now. Save you trouble.

An appointment with an orthopaedic surgeon was fixed for later that day.

—We'd like you to come in for a few days, said the surgeon.

—Into the hospital? asked Tosh incredulously.

—We want to take a closer look at the bone.

Tosh's whole sense of himself was radically altered by the prospect, as though he had turned around to find the back projection of his activities had, without his knowledge, cut from mournful drifting flotsam to a loud momentous traffic. Who would bring the magazine out, what about the play, the school kids, exams, the summer — even as they were all transformed into matters of crucial importance, he sensed the first faint intimation of some other force moving in, which could take the sum total of these passions and commitments and pinch them to a tiny smudge of red on the ball of the thumb.

He made an effort to catch up with the casual exchange of the conversation:

—How long for?

—Maybe a week. We'll need to stitch the leg and put a cast on it after we take the sample of bone.

Tosh summoned his moiling resources.

—Okay. When should I come in?

—We'd like you to stay here right now. There's a bed for you in Ward 18.

—No, said Tosh. No, that's not – it's impossible. I've a lot of business to clear up. I'd need to get some things together too.

—You could phone your family.

—No, I'll need to go, really.

—Fine. We want you in as soon as possible, though. Shall we say this afternoon?

—Well – what about after tea tonight, my father could bring me up. Around eight or so.

The surgeon looked quizzical.

—Yes, that'll do. We'll operate in the morning.

He walked amongst the traffic. You're keeping well ahead of me. They were always talking about your gift of free will, what's the hold-up? Expect the unexpected: sounds nice, means nothing. What to do? Ring the school, ring Harrison. He can tell her. No. Go up and have coffee and make methodical arrangements.

Drizzle outside, the coffee a kind of foamy drizzle, everybody packed in round the furrowed wooden tables, hunched in wet coats, windows steamed up, a clamorous fug. A student called McIlwaine was laughing, sitting amongst the theatre crowd on the edge of the stage. His laughing sounded at once forced and uncontrollable.

She brushed away rain sliding out of her hair.

—Why's he laughing, said Tosh.

She looked bemused, looking away.

—He does this all the time, pay no attention to him. It was a girl calling from near McIlwaine, his girl.

—He gives her cause for concern and she gives him concern, that's their relationship, said Tosh. No?

—He's mad, she said.

—He's got a glass eye, he only looks mad, said Tosh.

McIlwaine's laughter turned into broken words:

—Ward 18... was it... did you say 18?

—Right, said Tosh.

—Oh Jesus they do some terrifying damage in there! shrieked McIlwaine and the mirthless engine of his laugh resumed.

—I hate medicals, said Tosh. Just think of the ones you know besides him, you'll see what I mean. God preserve their future patients, he said, looking skyward.

Rain touched her thin mouth. She licked it away.

She's going to say she adores the taste of rain. She looks depressing on a day like this, the little white face all pinched, the skinny ankles under the shapeless coat and those cursed sodden flat-soled shoes. It has to end.

—Will I be able to visit you?

Her lip slightly fluttered, she gazed on at the coffee cup she was twiddling with.

—They said three days is probably all I'll be in. It's only a check-up to take a chip off the bone and analyse it.

She didn't speak. McIlwaine went on laughing.

✳

In the evening his father drove him forebodingly to the hospital with an overnight suitcase. They were shown into a dark side ward and stood awkwardly in the growing gloom. Two iron bedsteads were empty, one directly opposite the door, the other to the right of the door. In the far corner, screens were drawn, presumably around a third bed: subdued moaning and grunting came from behind the screens.

Tosh longed for his father to go; he could no longer sustain one other burden beside his own. At last the ward sister appeared, a dumpy honest lady in red uniform, and took his father away to sign a form. He sat on the edge of the bed to the right of the door, hands in his overcoat pockets, and watched the thin black shoe swinging on his left foot. Certainly he was being moved in some direction, but towards what destination? Too soon to think of an end, it had hardly started yet. He wondered if the groaning man were dying. Whatever that meant. His father reappeared with the sister to say a gruff, troubled good-bye.

—Now, Mr. Tosh, will you put these on for me, you can have the bed you're sitting on.

—Will I get into bed now, right away? said Tosh clumsily, it seemed so odd and irrevocable.

—Yes, of course. Leave your clothes in the case, we'll take care of them. She was a bit abrupt. She went out, leaving him with pale green briefs which tied at each side and a short white smock. Slowly he shed the street clothing which seemed now like an old elaborate disguise, put on the two stark garments of this new role, and sat in the bed in the twilight which was full still of the old man's wounded noises.

Presently two nurses appeared, black-haired, very youthful-looking and bearing a covered tray.

—You're going to get your leg shaved, the first said brightly, turning on the bedside lamp and adjusting its glow on to the bed.

They bent over the naked leg, which was stretched across the circle of light, scraping intently. From the shadows without, Tosh looked on.

—Who's behind the screens? he asked.

—It's an old man, said the first, who was the experienced one, murmuring guidance to the other, a novice. —He had his operation today, he's all right, it's just the anaesthetic, he's still coming round.

Tosh felt impelled to talk on, out of an obscure prompting to make them connect his leg with the rest of his being.

—You must get a pretty jaundiced view of people, being a nurse, he suggested with rather too much bravura in his voice. It was the wrong thing to say, apparently. An extra shade of briskness entered her voice which pushed it over into sounding patronising. They looked on nursing as a public service, they had great regard for their patients, she said. Tosh plunged on, trying to win her over with teasing.

—Watch you don't go down with the deadly Flo Nightingale syndrome, he warned, with less success than before. They finished up, covered their tray, and bore it away in high dudgeon.

They had shinned down the mooring rope, Tosh gashing his knuckles on the barnacles of the harbour wall.

—This here's the centre-plate, said Higgins proudly. You have to lower it before you put up the sail. Watch you don't let the wire slip out of your fingers.

—That wire's a bit crude isn't it? said Tosh. It wouldn't take much for the poxy thing to slip out and sink to the bottom.

Higgins was peeved by any affront to his dual capacity of proprietor and skipper. —You don't expect a luxury liner for thirty quid.

—I love it, said Tosh. It's got soul, it's got *duende*, a certain *je ne sais quoi*, a sort of *chutzpah*, a...

—Your arse, said Higgins. Here, stow this cover under the duckboards. Don't forget what I told you, Ready About and Lee-Ho.

—What's the duckboards? said Tosh slyly.

Higgins was hoisting the main sail. Braying yacht club voices gusted round the harbour walls. Suburban parents sat dumbly in their cars gazing out blindly over the harsh gaiety of the sea. The yacht sprang forward like a rush of blood.

—Crikey, said Higgins.

—We're heading straight for the frigging wall! yelled Tosh.

—Give us the tiller, ordered Higgins, lurching clumsily down the boat. —You hold on to the jib sheet and watch your head.

The yacht slewed round and accelerated diagonally towards the narrow harbour mouth.

—Gosh, said Higgins.

—We haven't a snowball's, muttered Tosh, mesmerised by the approaching gap with the gentle green swell rolling through it. They seemed to be travelling at about forty miles an hour. He closed his eyes. The yacht shot through the harbour mouth as though the harbour had spat it out. It plunged into the choppy open water, bobbed around, and slowed down. Tosh opened his eyes. Higgins was scratching the pimple on his nose.

—Ready about.

—Up your hole.

—We are the first that ever burst, recited Tosh.

—I'm getting a hernia.

—Into this silent sea.

—It's your turn to row.

Tosh stretched out his legs in mock luxury at the helm. —You've got exactly, let me see, yes, another nine minutes and fourteen seconds to go.

—What we want is a cushion for this centre-board. It's murdering my testimonials.

—Never worry. With the life you lead, you'll probably have to shed them in the autumn anyway.

Higgins guffawed in reluctant delight. Water streamed down silver from his raised oar blades. The still lough surrounded them like an empty auditorium, with the sun a thin disc of salmon in the western sky, and the moon a pallid crescent in the east. Tosh included it all in a sweeping gesture of his left arm, the right one draped languorously over the tiller.

—The slow machinery of the heavens, he said.

—What we want is to overtake a sleek flying fifteen, with two luscious dollies in it.

—Yacht club harlots. Content yourself with the august panoply of sky and ocean. Look at that sky, oh man! That there sky is cosmic mind, yawning its awning over…

—What about that thin thing, are you still poking her?

—Yawning its awning. Over our yearning.

—What?

—I'm still going with her. As she would put it. But not in any direction, as I would put it. Except down.

—As long as you're getting your oats.

—Even that paltry trinket is denied me. She's totally intacta. She's saving herself up for the man from the Prudential.

—Who?

—Mr. Security.

—Jesus. I hate that. Those scheming scrags that won't do a turn till after the engagement party.

—As you would put it.

They fell silent for a moment, each musing.

—My bollocks are destroyed, announced Higgins.

There was no wind, but a steady current of cool evening air was perceptible, as though the light were pouring gently down the throat of the horizon.

—Why do you not give her the push? asked Higgins.

—I don't seem to be very good at things like that.

—You? You're the smoothest mover I've ever seen. What about all those stories you've told birds?

—All in the past. I've stopped operating. I've ground to a halt.

—You're getting soft. You're getting too involved with your women.

—I'm getting less and less involved with everything.

The rose pink of the sun was flooding across the sea around them. Although they moved steadily across the water, the town and its harbour seemed to Tosh to keep at a steady distance from the prow.

—I'll tell you one thing, went on Tosh. How the hell you can carry on at the old routines, is beyond me. The thought of prowling after some wretched girl at a dance and fumbling with her buttons in the car – it depresses me beyond words.

—You've just lost your touch. You told me once you were mad to seduce every woman you met in the street.

—Certainly I did, I'm a dupe and a victim like everybody else. That's the organising principle of society, seduction, your parents seducing you from the day and hour you're born, your school seducing you, your church, then your employer, and reinforcing all those vested interests you've got a slimline cathode ray tube in the corner. It's a network of seductions every day of your life. I want out of it.

—I suppose you intend to pull yourself off in the toilet every night.

Their voices, animated now by the discussion, resonated across the vast empty amphitheatre.

—Surely there must be women, said Tosh, who want out the same as me. I'd give a lot to meet an attractive woman who didn't either ignore me or try to seduce me.

—You're a conceited bastard.

—Every seduction is mutual, you fool.

—That statement's nothing more than an intellectual turd and it's long past your turn to row, you sly bugger.

Higgins was shipping the oars as he spoke, standing up and rubbing his anus. Tosh, chuckling, edged slowly up the boat, settled himself astride the centre-board and took over the oars.

—You're totally blind to the extent of your own fantasies, he said.

—I've shagged three different hoors in the past fortnight, and there's no fantasy about that. It wasn't them that did the seducing, either, two of them were virgins and the third one was engaged to a solicitor.

—You treat women as conquests, and they think of you as a thrilling adventure, but it amounts in the end to nothing more than mutual masturbation.

—Now you're sounding like a minister teaching sex education.

Tosh laughed a little.

—Fair enough, but you're entirely aware that I'm very partial to masturbation. I just want to make sure that I'm getting the names of things right. I've no desire to confuse a woman with a slot-machine. Conversely, I can't put up a pretense of being the man from the Prudential.

—Why not just have a good time and shove all this half-baked philosophy.

—Did you ever get tangled up in seaweed when you were out swimming?

—Naw.

—Neither did I. But I feel as if my head's caught up in a clog of emotions like that, trying to pull itself free before it gets drowned.

He had settled into a steady pace of rowing, parallel with the rhythm of ideas he struggled to express.

—I think that everybody's in the same boat... if you think of your whole network of relationships... you're like a fly in a spider's web of neuroses... I want to hack free of all that mess... all that tangle of hurts and ploys you get enmeshed in... the whole painful charade of definitions and decisions... it'd be so idyllic to float free of it...

—That's just sentimental escapism.

—No, it's clinging to your neuroses that's escapism... that's how people identify themselves... all those fantasies like security and romantic love... they're all finally predatory, people are terrified of nourishing themselves... no sooner have you wrenched free from your mother... than you're desperately trying to get fouled up with a surrogate mother... you can't get involved in a mature way with other people... until you're completely involved in your own selfness... which means floating out on your own sea... and most people are scared to death at the thought... it's too real for them, not too escapist... anyway a good time is exactly what I'm dying for... but I don't see any prospect of it... short of a head amputation.

—There's a big freighter coming towards us, said Higgins.

Tosh looked over his shoulder. The peaceful spacious light seemed to have grown taut and angry round the enormous black hulk, bearing down on them like a lowering fortress.

—You didn't tell me! yelled Tosh. You stupid shit! What are you doing! Change course!

—It's all right, said Higgins. Keep rowing. Powered boats have to give way to sail.

—For Jesus' sake, shouted Tosh, we haven't even the sails up!

But already the great black shape was perceptibly veering. They watched its flank slide away.

—Crikey, said Higgins. It's really true, then – gives you a terrific sense of power, doesn't it.

—Look, whispered Tosh, gesturing feebly with his head.

A towering wall of water from the freighter's bow was creeping soundlessly towards them.

—My goodness, said Higgins.

Tosh woke up like a blind being raised to find a small male nurse with glasses and slightly hunched shoulders pulling the screens round his bed.

—I have to shave you for your operation.

—A couple of nurses shaved my leg last night, said Tosh. Then realised that it was his pubic hair the man meant. He lay rigid as the razor rasped dryly round his testes. There's a ritualism about it all, he thought. The cleansing and purification of the sacrificial victim. He looked down when the man had finished to where his penis lay disconsolate and wrinkled in the middle of a bald spotted ring of flesh. My pale confectioner. He had just settled himself again when another nurse came through the curtains. She was a fair-haired girl with freckles and a gap in her front teeth. She told him to turn over on his side, and injected him in the hip and told him that his mouth would begin to get dry after a while.

He lay and waited and wondered if the noun patient and the adjective patient were the same word: to be a patient, to be patient. To wait. Suffer whatever happens. Most people were patient. Most people lay in their patient beds and let it happen. Doctors seemed to evoke all the traditional Christian virtues from people, meekness, humility, patience. Not so much loving kindness. Doctors should run the churches instead of ministers and priests. You might argue every point with a teacher or a lawyer, but few people would answer their doctor back. Because of suffering. That was the authority they had recourse to. That was the sanction that shut everybody up. Most people were patients.

They helped him shift his drowsy body onto the trolley. Then ensued a phantasmal journey with curious faces floating by, with echoing voices and steps, the curved ceilings of long corridors gliding by, the flood-lights of the operating theatre with a ring of shifting eyes above white masks, a ring of tall white creatures peering down into him like quaint inquiring birds.

Little lady, in her hat, hat-pin: she won't go, *I can see, you're suffering*, let go, her eyes, *it's your leg, he told me*, glinting, *my son, he's down the ward*, let go, her eyes: talon, on my arm, *you might, face God*, powdered nose, *very soon*, let go, *have you thought, of that*, oh yes, her claw, her eyes, *let your thoughts, turn to Jesus*, oh please, she won't go: *the pain, we feel, on earth*, a nurse, *is nothing, to the pangs, of hell*, call a nurse, her face, white powder, *tell me son*, my arm, oh please, *do you love God?*, oh yes, oh yes, let go, she won't go, *do you love him?* Let it end, her hat, her breath, *do you show him, you love him?*: no no, please end, it hasn't, really started, oh go, *for he loves, you*, she doesn't, *you know*, she thinks, she's doing good, her hat-pin, glints, *will you pray*, she doesn't, *with me son*, know, oh please, she doesn't know, *Oh dear Jesus*, come quickly, a nurse, *who is, our only personal, Saviour*, no no, let it end, iron claw, oh my arm, cutting, cutting: *help us Lord to purge our sinful hearts of all that is wicked and rotten within them send thy cleansing fires to devour the vain and idle fancies of our minds and to eat up in its pure flame the filthy and vile habits and desires of our bodies and receive this boy into the healing light of thy redemption* no no no, hat eyes white claw claw breath, quick end please nurse won't go, let me let turn go away no no get quick oh Christ when when let go leave go go away please go.

The little lady bent over Tosh till the brim of her hat touched the counterpane under his chin.

—What is it, son, she said eagerly. Yes. Tell me what it is, what are you trying to say.

Her bright eyes darted bird-like, her small veined hand clamped tightly round his forearm.

—Please, he whispered. Please, my arm. You're hurting it. Please. You're hurting my arm.

That night he lay in the dark ward rubbing his right heel up and down the sheet twisting his head to right and left on the pillow. His left leg was no longer a dull marrowless shell, it had effloresced into a fire-ball, a swelling boil, an angry welling roar. They had crammed it into a cast like a heavy iron band from above the knee to the ankle, his foot felt like a gravid dark red balloon that soon would burst, he touched the livid skin of his thigh, it was drum-like. A nurse came, she looked at him and said she was going for the house surgeon. The house surgeon came and sent for the male nurse and gave him instructions. Tosh watched the male nurse arrive with giant clippers, the small hunched figure in white. The cold metal of the clippers pressed into the tender skin of his foot and then of his thigh as they sliced open the cast at top and bottom.

Within twenty minutes his right heel stopped grinding, his head ceased to twist. Sleep began at last to seep into the still recesses of his body. It took me over completely, he told himself. I'd forgotten pain. You always do, there's no way to remember it. My voice didn't stop, but it stuck in a groove. It screamed over and over the same things. That must be what madmen hear.

He had sat heavy and slow with drink in a corner of the sofa and the party had seemed to swivel round him. Stephens appeared from time to time, middle-aged lecturer in his anonymous grey suit, and his face graven with rigours of a long quarrel with life.

—You could do something with yourself, you young punk. You might. But you'll have to clear away all this shit and nonsense.

He was sodden, almost incoherent: he was moving away to a new post, this was his final contumacious fling, and all the repressed hungering down the years to insult the males and assault the females was finding a moderate realisation.

—What nonsense? said Tosh.

Stephens waved his arms about vaguely, seeming to take in everything that pertained to Tosh's life.

—Maybe you've got something. Maybe. Maybe you've got it. Let me know if you ever find out.

He lurched away and threw his arms round a tall red-haired girl and buried her mouth under a clumsy determined kiss.

A matronly woman with bright steady eyes and a permanent little smile clipped to her mouth sat with her hand on Tosh's arm, her face swaying close to him.

—You're young. You've got a lifetime in store for you, she said. It doesn't matter what you do with it. Doesn't matter. There's only one thing I want you to bear in mind. Just one.

She leaned in closer, her tepid scent pulsing over his face.

—Whatever you do, she said. Whatever you do, do it strong! Do it strong!

She squeezed his arm and was gone.

—This is a dying civilisation, he said to Prudence who kept returning to him on the sofa.

—You're drunk, she said.

—Think of average moments in the life of this culture. One person's worrying about being overweight. Somebody's feeding meat to their cat.

—You're delirious, she said.

—We keep trying to lose our selves. Impossible to live face to face with your own face, so you keep trying to drown it in each other's bodies, or music, drink, dope, anything but the void in your head.

—You're getting on like an evangelist . . .

Somebody had leaned over and was talking loudly into the far side of her face. Tosh talked on, to himself.

—There's neither self-love nor community in this room. It's another scene of slow break-down. There's nothing worth doing in this society, nothing. Your life's a wasted function. A bus ticket or an election poster or a milk carton.

He lay back, tiring of the performance.

Prudence was gone. The matronly woman was back again.

—You're young, she said. You probably haven't even discovered your true identity yet.

—I'm struggling to lose it, actually.

—The important thing is, she said, leaning in close, what you do with your life's of no account. You can be anything you like, doesn't matter. What matters is how you go about it. What matters is how you do it. I want you to remember me telling you this. Do it strong! If you follow through on that, you won't go wrong. Do it strong!

The surgeon had iron-grey hair and hefty shoulders and forearms. He was phlegmatic and imposing. He would have been equally as impressive as a jetliner pilot or a chairman of the board; a godman of Western Cities. Tosh felt himself sit up to attention in the presence of such authority.

—We've finished our tests on that bone sample, the surgeon said.

—Ah. Tosh cleared his throat.

—What you have is a species of tumour on the femur. The tumour's active and it could spread fairly rapidly. Some of these tumours can be arrested by treatment, but the only chance with others, like yours, is immediate surgery.

The surgeon's face was inscrutable. His voice was a gentle, uninflected murmur. Tosh's heart had begun to accelerate like a train.

—I'm afraid we'll have to take your leg off, said the surgeon.

It seemed too simple a way to put it. Tosh's heart was like a fish trying to jump out of his chest.

—You mean – amputation? he said foolishly.

—Yes, said the surgeon, in the same *sotto voce*, —I think the sooner the better. We were planning on tomorrow morning, if you agree to that.

—It'll kill my mother, said Tosh.

—Your mother knows already. She's taken it very well. I told your father three days ago.

Lunatic phrases were flashing into Tosh's mind. He wanted to say something ruefully ironic which would make the surgeon smile and calm the blood thundering between his ears. He almost said What the hell, at least I won't have to play football again. But he couldn't trust his voice not to crack and ruin it.

—Is there no other way? he said.

—At the present time there's no way that we know of. We don't even know what causes these tumours. You've said that you remembered being kicked a few times under the knee playing games as a youngster. That could have started off the trouble, but then again it might just have aggravated what was already there.

The surgeon talked on, about growing too fast, and strontium-90.

—What happens if you don't do it? said Tosh.

—It'll spread throughout your body if we don't stop it now. It may already have spread a bit, so we'll take the leg off in mid-thigh. I wouldn't ask you to agree to this if there was the slightest chance of saving the leg, believe me.

Tosh was aware that he was controlling himself in the surgeon's presence. It was head prefect psychology, he had to take it like a man, show the stuff he was made of. He wondered what was going on behind the granite composure of the surgeon, who was talking now about artificial limbs.

—You'll be able to lead an entirely normal life. The limbs they make these days are practically indistinguishable from the real thing. I know it must be a great shock. It'll take time to get used to the idea. But it's not the end of your life. There's no reason why your life should be changed at all. You'll be able to return to your studies, there's virtually nothing that you've been doing up to now that you won't be able to go on doing.

—Thanks, doctor. A part of Tosh was appalled at the fatuousness which fearful news seemed to be provoking from him.

—Your father and brother are outside. Will I let them come in now, or do you want a few minutes alone?

—It's okay. Send them on in.

His father seemed small and ashen after the massive presence of the surgeon. There were a few tiny flecks of white on his brother's lips. Tosh felt a fake theatricality taking him over to keep things operational.

—Well, it's not as bad as it might be, he said. I half expected it, to tell you the truth. I'm lucky that it's the kind that can be stopped. How's ma?

—Oh, she's grand, said his father hoarsely. She was shocked a bit at first – you know – we all were.

—It's helped her to forget her own troubles, said his brother.

They talked on alertly, briskly, like a film slightly speeded up. The ward sister came in in the middle of it and added her own deft touches of reassurance. —They can work wonders with these new metal limbs. They really can. Then his father and brother went away with the sister. Then a nurse came in with his tea. She approached him almost fearfully, her face full of distress. The meal was scrambled eggs on toast.

—I'm sorry – about the news, she said.

—What the hell, at least I'll never have to play rugby again, said Tosh.

She pulled the trolley across the bed and the smell of the toast and eggs filled his nostrils.

—I don't think I can…

—Try to eat a bit, go on. You won't have anything in the morning. Just take what you can, I'll leave it here.

He lifted the fork and realised his hands were trembling violently, and were stone-cold. He put a blob of the yellow matter into his mouth and his stomach heaved. He put the fork down gingerly and pushed the trolley away and swallowed the blob of egg very slowly.

—Is the leg to come off? said the old man in the corner bed.

—Yes.

—I thought that from what you were saying. That's hard lines, son.

—Yeah.

Other nurses came in, fearful and distressed, in ones and twos, to offer condolence. The evening was taking on aspects of a ritual processional.

When it was finally clear that he was alone, Tosh became filled with a profound calm. There was an almost inhuman clarity in his mind, his head felt rinsed, he was imbued with a limpid serenity. Unknown was the only word for what was facing him. It might be death. Whatever that meant. It would certainly be some form of death. He pushed back the bed-clothes and placed his left leg on top of them. He wouldn't be the same person after they took it away. A quarter of him would have disappeared. He studied the leg intently, memorising it. From thigh to ankle it looked sick and defeated, with its wasted muscles and white hairlessness and the six-inch vertical scar down the front crossed at intervals by stitch-marks, like a cartographer's railway line. But the foot clearly wanted to live. It was forlornly expressive like an eager dog staring into the muzzle of its master's shotgun. Its nails were slightly yellowed and needed trimming. An ancient fossilised corn rounded out the smallest toe. It was obvious why feet had never ranked high in the aesthetics of the human anatomy, they were its faintly comic antipodes, its point of contact with the soil. For all that there was a harmony of line and proportion at which Tosh marvelled.

He pondered on where they would take the leg, what they would do with it. Medical students would practice on it, probably. Maybe McIlwaine would dissect it, laughing insanely. At any rate, it would have preceded the other three quarters of his ailing animal into the purely vegetable and mineral existence of dead matter. Or into the consciousness of which all matter partakes. Or into a spot from which it could conveniently fly out to be reunited with its hip on the Day of Judgement. It was generally assumed that a faith in such convictions was essential to face ordeals of suffering and death with equanimity. Yet Tosh felt entirely composed, and certain of nothing except for his own blind ignorance. The only resource he was aware of was the voice in his head itself, the fact of his own consciousness, and it was telling him that tomorrow when the knife and the saw went in, it itself would be drowned in gristle and blood and then he would have no resources at all. The fear created by such a prospect was an experience which entirely transcended the familiar everyday emotion which had frequently loosened his bowels and dried his mouth. It was a state of emotional refrigeration which had created the almost preternatural calm in which his thoughts were ordering themselves so composedly.

He was aware of taking conscious pleasure in the rational processes of his mind for the first time in his life, just as he had perceived the shapeliness of the human foot for the first time. He would be deprived of both of these attributes tomorrow morning. His life had been remarkable to nobody but himself up to this point, and to him it had been a fretted, directionless affair, crowded with other people whom he could never know, who rose and fell like skittles in their unhappy dealings with one another and with him. That existence was at its solitary climax now for him, and for them it was already over, if they ever saw him again he would not be the same person. He had a powerful sense of having reached the end of his growing. The growth was cankered. If the canker could be excised, he would have arrived at last at the unknown life which he was destined to live. It would be his own life and he would have to live it with whatever resources were available. In the meantime a wave as tall as a ship was creeping soundlessly towards him over the dark water.

Tosh woke early in the morning from a drugged sleep. He felt exactly as he had the previous night, except that he knew his introspection before the event was completed and his mind needed work to do.

He fished out a notebook and ballpoint from the locker. By the time the pethidine had begun to stupefy him, he had written a fair-sized essay on the state of poetry in contemporary society. Years later, he wondered what had become of the essay. He never saw it again.*

When they wheeled him into the theatre, the surgeon was standing drying his hands on a towel and smiling at him. He observed this and the alert eyes of the anaesthetist as the needle entered his arm with a vivid sense of a detachment that was now total.

Much later, Gillespie, a stringy medical student with hair flopping over his intense face and a rough cockerel neck, came in for his liver to be operated on. In the afternoon, Tosh went down the wards and stood at his bedside.

—Not too good, Pete?

—Bloody torture. The narrow face, weakly naked without its spectacles, twisted ceaselessly on the pillow, sweat beading the ashen cheeks and forehead.

After several days he was well enough to visit Tosh. He draped himself on the edge of the bed, in the hospital's striped green towelling dressing-gown, and strummed the guitar.

—My back gets covered in pimples during the winter, he was saying. Yours must be worse, lying sweating in bed for a couple of months. The only way to get rid of them is to burn them off in the sun during the summer.

—I never look, said Tosh.

—What about that? He nodded towards the mound in the bed-clothes.

---

* Parker's final plan for the novel, not realized in all its particulars, indicates that he envisaged an additional section to go after this one, likely representing Tosh's essay. For more information about this, see the textual note and Appendices 3 and 4.

—Not bad. Bearable. If they leave it alone.

—Any secondaries?

—What?

—Any sign of secondary deposits?

Something obscene began to wriggle onstage in Tosh's mind but a curtain fell abruptly across it.

—No. Not as far as I know.

—If they haven't found any you're okay. Here, entertain me on this thing, I can only play a couple of chords.

—How long does it take before there's no... before you're clear...

—Dunno with your thing. About seven or eight years probably.

—I thought the amputation was all it took. I mean, I thought I could at least forget about that now.

—You probably can. Who was the surgeon?

Tosh told him.

—Good bloke, said Gillespie. His voice was casually abrasive. —Of course the main requirement for amputating is just brute strength. A brawny right arm. You know how they do it?

—The funny thing is, said Tosh, I've never given it a thought. In all the struggle to cope with it.

—They mark it out and slice the skin some distance below where they want to chop it. Then they peel the skin back, like a banana. Then they have to cut carefully through the sinews and muscles to keep as much intact as possible. But when they're down to the bone there's nothing for it but the old hack-saw, and putting the shoulder into it. It's no different from three hundred years ago. Of course speed was what counted then. Most patients died under the shock of it before anaesthetics. After the limb's severed they just peel the skin flaps down and stitch them. It doesn't take that long.

—You've watched it?

—I wasn't able to watch it, actually, said Gillespie. His long hands, drooping and tapered moved restlessly around, pushed the flop of hair off his forehead. —Not the first time, I had to leave. I've seen it since, though.

They came to visit Tosh, sometimes singly and often in clumps. Once when the sister wasn't around he counted nine figures in a horseshoe round the bed. People came whom he hadn't seen for years. Others whom he'd been seeing every day never came. Increasingly he noticed how they talked more to each other, less to him. When the nine were there, they carried on several criss-cross dialogues simultaneously, one about a current film, one about an exam, one about charter flights. He lay examining their faces and voices in agitated motion above him, in the upper world of thrusting elbows and jet planes rending the sky. Occasionally their kindly smiling eyes took him in as a regrettable fact. He and they belonged now to two different kinds of real life and there was no point of contact, an invisible magnetic field was pushing between, keeping the distance constant. Really, the whole business of hospital visiting was very odd. The atmosphere in the wards prior to visiting time was that of the nursery when cold baths have been ordered. Yet Tosh resented those who didn't come. Visitors, on their part, seemed to derive most of their pleasure from the effort they made to get to the hospital. They gave gifts to the patients as they gave tips to taxi-drivers, out of a routine sense of obligation. A pile of cigarette cartons beside the bed reached to Tosh's shoulder. The bottles of orange, lemon, grapefruit and blackcurrant drinks, which left a harshness in his throat, he passed on to his mother, along with most of the fruit and the chocolates and the stationery and the handkerchiefs. The books filled his locker, unread.

*

She hung around after the bell rang, the others slipped out discreetly.

—I never can talk to you, she said. There's always so many people. I can't be on my own with you.

—You're on your own with me now.

—There's no time to talk now.

He didn't want to be on his own with her or anybody. He didn't want to 'talk'. That talking in particular had been done enough times already; so had all talking in general, as a valuable activity. Two voices were grinding him to the point of break-down, one at the red mouth of his severed thigh and the old one in his head. Their endless vituperation was all the dialogue he could contain.

—I don't want the summer job, she was saying, trembling on the verge of tears. —I won't see you for ten weeks if I go.

He saw with relief a nurse hovering at the door.

—There's no problem, he said. You need to get away. Just get out into the sun, put me out of your head. You'd better go. He indicated the nurse.

—Bye-bye, Prudence.

She kissed him tremulously and was gone. She'll be back for another try, his head assured him. I can't face it.

She came on a non-visiting afternoon when he was out on the veranda, sitting with Tony and some of the men from the main ward. They looked at her surreptitiously, not talking except for the odd truncated remark.

—Can we not go up to the ward? she whispered.

—It's nice and sunny here, he said.

She had dressed up for the visit, her body looked frail and delicately wrought in a way that had often excited his senses. But the corners of her mouth and eyes were pulled down with an abject pleading which threw his mind into a silent fury, he kept on his dark glasses, looking out over the lawn away from her tiny white face.

—My flight goes tomorrow afternoon, she said.

—Great. You'll have a tan by the end of the week, you're dead lucky.

—I don't feel lucky.

—You will when you get there.

—Ever since I knew… you wouldn't be going… I haven't wanted to go at all.

His cigarette was nearly finished, he lit a new one.

—I want to talk privately, she said.

—It's okay here.

—Could we not go up to the ward. Please, she whispered miserably.

He pulled deeply on his cigarette and stubbed it out. —All right, he said, standing up and thrusting his forearms into the clamp of the metal crutches.

He had just got through the glass doors into the main ward when the left crutch cracked and he lurched down, twisting to fall on his backside and not on the stump. He felt sick. For a fraction of time his reflexes had caused him to throw his weight onto a leg that wasn't there. He was lucky to have nothing worse than skinned knuckles and a sense of confused decorum. She was helping him up, a nurse was bringing up a wheelchair.

—He's getting far too fat, said the nurse breezily, with all that rich food. You'll need to give that chair a good hard shove, wait till you see.

He was shaken and on edge. This is beyond her wildest ambitions, pushing me in a wheelchair, what more could she ask for. From the rows of beds on each side, the old men smiled and nodded.

When they got to the ward, he stripped off his green plaid dressing-gown and got into bed, and lit a cigarette. She pulled the screens partially round the bed.

—What the hell? he said.

—In case anybody comes in.

He leaned back on the pillows and closed his eyes.

—You know what it is, I want to talk about, she started. About…

you and me. I've been so worried. I've been going over and over, in my mind, what you said to me last week. Put me out of your head. I thought at the time you just meant, to not worry about you during the summer but have a good time. But the way you said it... I suddenly saw it could mean, you wanted me to forget entirely.

His head ranged across continents of encyclopaedic rumination while she spoke, vast tundra wastes of philosophical speculation, mountain ranges of social and political theorising, dense virgin forests of numerical calculation, interstellar voids of spiritual exploring, while the grinding jaws at his stump also roared away. The sun outside made the ward seem gloomy, the screens were a double gloom, he felt sweat on his face, he was going under. Her voice was snagging on buried sobs, she had stopped talking, she was biting her lower lip.

—I'm wordless, he muttered. His throat burnt. —I don't have any words. You'll just have to manage without any words. I can't offer you any words.

He poked at her hand. She put her face into his shoulder and an arm over his chest. He folded his own elbow over the arm and turned exhausted eyes up to the ceiling. The blind was three-quarters drawn to keep the sunlight out. Through the remaining gap a harsh white fuzz of light bore down. He wanted to gulp the smoke of his cigarette, but his right arm was gently pinioned by her small trunk. There was no way up. Her hair moved across his vision, her tiny mouth was pressing on his.

—I'm frightened, she said. Her damp face was pressed into his neck. —It's been so terrible without you. I can't stand the thought, of ten weeks without even seeing you.

—It's all right, his mouth affirmed, It'll be fine. His mouth was on its own now, and could make any noises it wanted, for if your telephone line's been severed, what does it matter what you choose to speak into the mouthpiece? Any soothing lies will do. —You'll be back in no time, he said loudly. I'll write to you every day. Come on, cheer up. He heard Tony coming into the ward. If I can hold out a few more minutes, she'll go. She won't come back. I'll write.

She moved away from him, but sat on, in silence. Tony was shuffling around, dropping his crutches. If she stays any longer he'll fart and cry out for a bed-pan. The sister suddenly appeared, looked askance at them and started pushing the screens back without a word.

—She's just going, sister, said Tosh.

—It's outside visiting hours, you know, said the sister sternly, walking out without looking at Prudence.

—You'd better head out, he said. Still she did not move. Then she reached for her bag and took out a present for him, obviously a record.

—They hadn't got the guitarist you talked about, she said. But I talked to the man in the shop and he said you'd like this.

—Yeah. That's terrific. Thanks for that.

She was definitely winding up now to leave. She had had her catharsis and now he could almost see her winding up the inner spring behind a brave face.

—I'll send you a card as soon as I get there, she said. He thought of all the times he had been through this scene before. He had always played it before but this time he hadn't played it. Always before at this point he had come up with a deflating gag which had caused the other person to smile and giggle through their tears and then they hugged and went off both feeling warm and recreated. He wondered if his mouth would do it, but it didn't. Now that release from the strain was so close, his whole being was rapidly nearing the burst. She looked one look of utter desolate misery, and then brushed him on the cheek and then was gone.

—She might as well have brought her nightie and stayed for the week-end, said Tony.

—Yeah. Tosh was in a mental swoon but his body seemed to be crashing round a livid cage, wild for some outlet.

Tosh hadn't helped his case with the Productions Committee by arriving twenty-five minutes late to present it. Normally it was hard to find anybody prepared to direct a play for the festivals. This year three students had put forward their names and ideas.

—What do you plan to call this effort? said McIlwaine sneeringly, his squinting eyes flashing.

—I thought I'd call it *What Is the Ocean Doing?*, said Tosh. It's a line from the poem.

—Tell us in detail how you envisage it, said the president.

—Well, everybody knows the narrative in *The Ancient Mariner*.

—Water water everywhere and not a drop to drink, that's all I know from it, said McIlwaine. We're not all bloody literature students, you know.

Tosh sighed. Already his will to argue the case for the production was ebbing.

He had thought of the idea only the previous week and had got no further than acting it out for Harrison on the stage of the Drama Hut.

—First of all, a wedding procession. The guests all flushed and beery, following the bride round the stage. She's flirting with them. You build up erotic excitement, slightly dangerous.

—Why not start it with the albatross?

Tosh moved to the front of the stage.

—No, no, I want the emphasis off the albatross. I don't think the crime interested Coleridge that much, it's the punishment. You remember what that was.

—They get becalmed and die of thirst.

—The crew dies but the Mariner is won in a game of dice by Life-In-Death. Remember the two hags in the translucent spectral boat dicing for him? What a scene – think of it! Anyway, the point about the life-in-death curse is that the penance involved goes on for the rest of the Mariner's life. Here it's here, listen to this:

Forthwith this frame of mine was wrenched
With a woeful agony,
Which forced me to begin my tale;
And then it left me free.

Since then, at an uncertain hour,
That agony returns:
And till my ghastly tale is told,
This heart within me burns.

Now that is the central point, I reckon. The confessional fever.

—Remorse.

—Not just that, but the child who has to blurt out the nightmare to his mother. It's the obsessive need to rehearse your memory of hell. If you don't enact it from time to time, it'll rend out your heart. That's the artistic impulse.

—Well. Go ahead with your staging.

Tosh moved upstage again, arms akimbo.

—Right you've got a big billowing cyclorama and it's all bright yellow midsummer lust in this opening scene. The guests all in navy blue suits and brown shoes and sweaty red faces and leering and pulling at the bride. Drums building it up. Then just when they're gathered round her and you can't see her and you're titillated at what might be going on in there, zap. They fall back to reveal the Mariner. He's young but he looks entirely devastated.

—Wait a minute. You can't have a young ancient mariner.

—He's got the long beard and the glittering eye, and the skinny hands – he's got the trappings of age, but he's obviously a young man underneath. He's scary, they can't take their eyes off him. He's possessed. Now the point of having a bunch of guests instead of just the one is that the Mariner forces them to re-enact his story. He doesn't just tell them about it. He puts them through it.

—What happens to the bride?

—She goes offstage to the wedding feast. Every so often you hear the music and laughter from that drifting in, and the guests are distracted by it. But he keeps mesmerising them back again. He describes the boat, the white foam flying, then the storm and the great ice floes – lightning, the cyclorama whipping about like a sail, thunder-sheet. Then the weird greens and blues of the ice. The guests are the other crew members, right? They mime the sailing of the ship.

—You could have rigging, in a kind of abstract cage-like thing across the stage.

—Right, they could climb it. So the next thing is the albatross.

—That'll be tricky. You're bound to suggest the old music-hall joke of firing into the flies and a bunch of chicken feathers fluttering down.

—No, the albatross can be just a talisman. As far as the sailors are concerned, it's just an omen of luck – good or bad according to the circumstances. The Mariner shoots it out of an entirely obscure impulse to challenge the prevailing superstition. He believes in it himself, maybe that's why it rebounds on him. What I'm saying is, it doesn't have to be a bird, it can be a figure-head, or a good luck charm nailed to the mast which he tears off and throws overboard.

Harrison was shaking his head.

—Won't work. The audience won't have any idea of what's happening.

—Okay, the alternative is to present the albatross as dark wing shadows which the Mariner can wrestle with in mime.

—I like that better.

—So he kills it. And they ostracise him. They put the mark of Cain on his forehead. Then the ship gets becalmed. The cyclorama droops. Hot and copper sky, the bloody sun at noon. The auditorium filled with noises of water. Mouths crusting over. The Mariner on the rigging, bites his arm, sucks red blood and cries 'A sail!'. The Skeleton boat moves across the cyclorama and the two women throw dice. Life-In-Death wins and she climbs on to him and he lets out an unmerciful scream. Then the women disappear and you get the terrible deaths of the crew. They all die in grotesque shapes – tongues out like swollen tripe, limbs contorted, but they all have their eyes fixed on the Mariner who has a fierce white light following him as he tries to hide. By now you've got complete stylisation. Hallucinatory. Eyes glowing in the flies. Great fronds and tendrils growing out from the wings. Deafening sounds of beating wings. Blood forming on the stage. A light show of melting faces on the cyc. In the middle of all this is a little bit of dancing coloured light. The sea snakes. The Mariner kneels before this. He blesses it. Zap; everything stops, ordinary moonlight. The crew stirring, taking their places like sleepwalkers. The ship sails on at preternatural speed – sea flashing by on the cyc. You hear the harbour bell, then three of the guests who've been in the wedding feast all this time come on as the pilot and the pilot's boy and the hermit. The hermit's a priest, and the pilot's a civil servant with an umbrella and briefcase. When they appear, the phantom crew line up with the Mariner in front. There's a great thundering crack, blackout, roaring water, then the Mariner's head and shoulders lit, struggling, clawing, then he's in the pilot boat and the pilot's boy's been unhinged and he's laughing. The two pillars of society are appalled by this apparition of the abnormal and they offer him no help at all. But he gets to the land and he falls down weeping for joy and the crew has all turned back into wedding guests. So he tells them what he's learned:

> *He prayeth well, who loveth well*
> *Both man and bird and beast.*

Then the bride appears again and other members of the wedding party. They're all gorging down food and groping at each other and the booze is flowing round among the guests and they all get sweaty faced again. The bride gets passed around too. It's society's idea of a love feast, greedy, violent, male contempt and female vanity. They brawl their way offstage leaving the Mariner on his knees with the wing shadow over him. Curtain.

Tosh kept the kneeling position with head bowed for a few minutes and then got up and joined Harrison in the auditorium.

—What do you think?

Harrison adopted his usual exaggerated gestures of serious thought, puckering his brows, stroking his sideburns, pulling quickly at his cigarette.

—Could work, could just work, he said. There are two points, though. One, I think that what you've got is essentially a show for children. That's where it would really score. Two, you haven't a snowball's with the Productions Committee. They won't touch an experimental show for the festivals. They'll go for the forty-seventh production this year of *Man For All Seasons*.

Tosh sat down. He was familiar enough with Harrison's psychology to anticipate remarks which would minimise the value of his ideas with just sufficient truth to demoralise him. Like all the tactics of Harrison's egomania, it made him smile inside. Even so, he felt deflated. The smaller his store of energy grew, the more vulnerable it seemed to be to depletion.

—I'm not going to argue it point by point, he said to the Productions Committee. You've got the whole idea. It would be an original show, something of our own instead of the usual aunts and uncles effort. It would be a gamble, like anything else worth getting into. We've got all the resources to do it.

The faces looking intently at the doodles burgeoning over their sheafs of paper gave him a clear answer.

*

He opened his eyes. A gaggle of white coats. At the foot of the bed. Staring at him. Crothers the head surgeon.

—Are you a revolutionary? said Crothers through his bifocals. The medical students grinned.

—I'm asleep, said Tosh. They want to amputate my hair. Crothers looking at his chart. Self-important little shit. Lecturing the medics. Big gaggle follow him from bed to bed, rigid in fear of his cutting tongue, ready with obedient laughter.

Opened his eyes again. His surgeon, leaning over. House doctor, sister. Taking swabs, oh no. Six-inch swab sliding deep into the wound, oh Jesus. Stinging. Deep. His mouth stretched wide. Going to be sick. Drawing it out. Hold on. It's gone. Murmuring.

Opened eyes. Surgeon looking down. Strong smile.

Opened. Slid down again. They're coming. Male nurse. Nurse. One at each arm.

—Good morning!

—I'm all right, said Tosh. Don't need pulled up.

—It'll only take a second, Mr. Tosh, and then you'll be comfortable for the rest of the day. He braced. Teeth clenched. Eyes closed. She fluffs up pillows. Strips down clothes. Lifts out cage. Hands in his armpits. They count. One, two, three: NOOOO...

—There you are, isn't that better. Swooned in a storm of animal hell. He pants, eyes staring, he closes them. Breathing easing. It's over, till tomorrow. Cage back. Clothes up. Long day to grind through.

The pain made a noise like *stoon stoon*. It had different gears. Sometimes a low maddening groan. Sometimes a deafening whine. Before they removed the drains from the wound they gave him a morphine shot which made it switch from low to high. Then they wheeled him into the examination room opposite the ward and put him on the table.

Then the sister took off his bloodily crusted bandages for the first time, and they were stuck to the stump, and the hell storm broke out and then the doctor removed the drains and he thrashed about and twitched in an agony of derangement.

Tosh opened his eyes again. Some engine snarling from outside. Some drill. His own engine labouring uphill. A minute passed. The drill girning, tearing into something. Deafening. A minute passed. His tortured blood answering to the wail of it. Mounting ratio of pain.

Another minute passed. This can't go on. Drilling into his head like a crazed dentist. Wound stretching open. Straining uphill. The seconds moved by. He pressed the button. Got to have a shot. Must be weeks now since. She won't give it to me now. Getting hooked. A minute went by. Drill searing on one wavering note.

The nurse loomed up.

—Yes, Mr. Tosh?

—I need an injection, nurse.

—Is the pain bad again.

Again?

—It's bad, yes.

—I'm afraid I'm not allowed to give you any more jags but I'll get you some tablets. Just hold on.

She's going to give you three aspirin. Kiss and make it better. Rub it with a docken leaf. Hold it under a cold tap.

—Here you are.

—I really need a shot, nurse. Please, for God's sake.

—I know how it must feel, but it's far too dangerous for you. Go on, take these. They're very strong. They'll help you.

Glass to his lips. Swallowed.

—What's the noise?

—We're getting a new entrance door fitted to the ward.

—Will they be at it for long?

—A couple of hours should see them through it. Try and get some sleep.

The drilling would sing in his blood like a stripped nerve, and then stop. There would be hammering. Then it would resume, goading the tormenting buzz in his slowly twisting body till his eyes ached in their sockets for lack of tears. The only landmark was visiting time. Surely it would stop then.

His mother and aunt came to visit. It didn't stop.

—That's a disgrace, said his aunt. Right outside that wall.

—Has it been going on for long? his mother asked.

—Yes, he said.

—They could at least have stopped it during visiting hours, said his aunt. I can hardly hear myself speak.

He turned over, there was a boy in a candy-striped dressing-gown looking at him.

—What have you got, are you a bone graft case? Richard, you call me.

Epicene. Great squat head with tufted wiry dark hair. Slob mouth.

—What's the clothes held up like that for? He held up the bedclothes to peer under. —You've no leg, what happened your leg.

—Leave him alone, said Joey.

—They've took away he's leg.

—Bugger off, will you, said Joey. Nobody wants you in here.

—I can go where I want. The nurses all know me. They give me injections for my mind. Hormones, you call them. But they've made me grow diddies on my chest.

Joey scoffing. The boy flares up.

—I have so. See this, if you don't believe me.

Pulls back the dressing-gown. A small perfect female breast on the sloping flabby chest. He vaunts it. Smirking.

—They don't know what to do with them. They think they'll have to remove them. That's why I'm in Ward 3. I could show you plenty more.

Nurse. Two nurses.

—Richard how did you get in here?

His face in triumph. —I told you they all knew me!

She making up the third bed, with the other nurse. She tousled auburn curls. Scolding.

—Get you back to your own ward. You were told not to wander. I'll tell matron on you, I will.

He jaunty. —I saw you and your boyfriend out on the lawn.

—Go to your ward. Do you hear me.

—I know when you're having your periods.

She flushed. Making bed with her head down.

—Do what I tell you and no more nonsense.

He feeling her buttock, she shrieks. —Stop that!

—Show them your diddies. Grabs at the strap of her uniform. She angrily pushing him away. He catches her arm. Twists.

—I showed them. Want to see them? Other nurse pulls him away. He dangerous, shrieking. —Leave me alone! You can't do anything on me. I'm a mental case.

She flustered, afraid. —If you don't go back to your bed this minute, I'll call for matron. He advances, she steps back.

—I don't know your name. Give us a kiss, nurse. Lunges at her arm. Twists it. Other nurse struggling with him. First nurse trying to avert face from the wet slobmouth kisses. Suddenly breaks off.

—Who's this bed for?

—Go away! Other nurse pushes, pummels him out.

Hot smothering air. Chocolate bar melted on the locker of the salesman.

—Here, wait till you see. Wait'll you see this. The life and soul

64

of the party. Thin hair glossy with oil. Lewd conspiratorial face. He brings out a toilet roll.

—This is a good one. Wait till you see the face on that wee nurse.

Smears the melted chocolate on the squares of toilet roll. Strews the floor with the crumpled brown-stained toilet paper.

—Nobody laugh. Just act natural. Watch her face.

The nurse comes in. Sees the toilet paper.

—What in heaven's name is this? Starts to pick it up. Blushing.

—How did this get here? Is this your big idea of a joke?

Loud laughing. Shrieking.

Joey hit a biscuit tin. Tosh strummed a guitar. The labourer with the broken finger sang along. Each in his own bed. Then they stood on the beds. Tosh stood on his one leg, thumping the guitar. Joey stood holding out his foot with the big toe missing, and banged on the biscuit tin. The labourer stood with his finger held upright in a cast, baying harshly. The song disintegrated into a formless racket.

An Indian doctor appeared in the door. They looked at him, silent.

—Please, do not stop, he said. It is very nice. He disappeared.

They fell down on the beds gagging on laughter.

Amidst the howl of the pain, he grew aware of his toes overlapping one another and clenched tight, he would have to untangle them and straighten them out. But they wouldn't budge. He strained at them but there was nothing. It was an itch that couldn't be scratched. It was a phone ringing and ringing that wouldn't be answered. You have no toes. But I can feel them there, twisted and squeezed together. I've got to flex them. The need rose to engulf him, he frantically tried to snag his mind on some other hook. Still the feel of the stiff cramped foot goaded him to madness. There is no foot. It's the nerves tricking you. Think about something else. Pay no attention to it. Don't, don't let it get control.

He sat on the veranda with Joey, their crutches leaning on the railing like submachine guns, pointed across the lawns.

—There goes that night nurse with the hips, said Joey.

—Pick her off.

—Pckh, pckh, pckh. Nobody leaves here alive.

The stern Baptist nurse storming in. Joey and Tosh drowsily singing.

—You two have been drinking! Trembling with the outrage of it. —You've been smuggling liquor into this hospital! You needn't think we don't know about it. What's in that bottle? Give me that bottle!

—That's sarsparilla, miss. That's a sarsaparilla bottle. See? Joey indicating the label.

—Give me the bottle.

—Leave his sarsparilla alone. Tosh muffled under the pillows. She turns on him.

—You've an operation in the morning. A fine time to get drunk. And you've both been smoking too. The air in here's like a... a nightclub!

—Hands off the sarsparilla.

—I want that bottle please. It's going straight to the matron. You'll hear more about this.

She wrenches the bottle away. She opens it. She sniffs it. She tastes it. She looks discomfited.

—Well you've just been lucky this time. Don't think you can always get away with it as easy as this.

Tosh looks out from the pillows.

—He demands an apology.

—That's right. Joey receiving back the bottle of sarsaparilla. —I definitely demand an apology. She goes out without a word, blinking rapidly.

The swabs showed an infection. They would have to reopen the wound. He got the injection at eight in the morning. At ten they told him the operation was postponed due to an emergency case. The injection had been a stiff one. He had begun by rising slowly from the bed till he was suspended six feet above it. Fast flowing warm water laved his body. Then cigarettes were between his fingers and as he languorously touched them to his lips and inhaled they filled him with interior caresses. Then he had to stop and lie entirely still, for every small movement racked him with uncontrollable mute laughter as though his whole body were suffering pins and needles. Then even the thought of a movement triggered the waves of paralysing laughter.

The first images were bone joints, knuckles, elbows, knees reeling by his open eyes, after a while they began to appear dislocated, arthritic, and then disembodied wounds appeared like mouths in fetid air, some mouthing obscenely at him some biting at him some growling flatulently at him. His body tingled as though from electric current. He touched his finger-tips to his forehead and they came away dripping.

The workmen had to replace the blind on the window in the ceiling above his bed. Their ladder straddled the bed. He watched them move above him like the awkward creatures of an alien world. The old blind was rotted and crumbling. Coarse flakes of grime drifted down to smudge the starched sterile frailty of his lineaments.

When they had wheeled Tosh back from the operating theatre, they had put a rubber sheet under the stump to keep the blood from staining the mattress and a structure like a birdcage over it to keep the bed-clothes from touching it. Then two nurses sat, one on each side of the bed. As his groans started to surface, one bathed his lips with cold water and the other dried the sweat erupting from his face.

He had become aware of the sweat erupting from his face. He had become aware of the organs erupting from his body. Everything in his body was trying to force an exit to escape the howling rage of his leg severed while still growing. He had become aware of his groaning and of a voice, his voice, saying to the two nurses, I'm sorry, I'm sorry.

The nurses were gone. Harrison was there. He was holding copies of the magazine, which had just been printed. He was speaking. He wasn't sure if Tosh was awake or not: the eyes were open but they weren't blinking and there was no response to Harrison's conversation. Tosh was in a new dimension beyond messages. He saw Harrison and the magazines as though through the eye of a fish. He lay like a long still fish in the murk at the bottom of a tank. He lay there out of time and space, submerged in a fluid that dissolves language and touching, entirely alone with himself, at last.

The Reverend Palmerston Boyle's voice boomed and growled like catarrh in the muffled lugubrious way it had echoed through the Sundays of Tosh's childhood. He was praying like a walrus and Tosh's parents were at the other side also on their knees.

His uncle was there. Putting his hand on Tosh's brow. The brute hand pushed Tosh's head into the pillow, into the mattress. Through the bed, into the floor. Slowly through the floor. Its tonnage kept increasing. Tosh needed to shriek out at his uncle's battered hang-dog face but he was beyond such signs of recognition.

A large white powdered nose and a hat-pin were there.

—I can see how you're suffering, said the old small lady. I heard about your poor leg from my son, down the ward there. Yes. We're all praying for you, child.

Her violet-veined hand closing round his supine wrist. His heel stirring.

—The whole church is offering a prayer to almighty God for the sake of your soul. He'll take you into his grace, child, if you'll only open your heart to Him. You might be face to face with Him in a very short time, if He so wills. Yes.

The nose and hat-pin closing in, the breath hot on his cheek.

—Have you thought about that, son? Have you? His mercy is infinite, but His wrath is terrible. And the sufferings of this world are as naught compared to the everlasting agonies of Hell, which burn yet do not devour.

His heel grinding, her hand tightening.

—But it's never too late to turn to Him. No. It's not too late to cast out all worldly sins of the flesh and accept the Lord Jesus into your heart. Do you love the Lord Jesus, son? Do you love Him? And do you show Him that you love Him?

Her fingers cutting.

—Will you pray with me? Will you? Oh dear Jesus who is our only personal saviour, help us to purge our sinful hearts of all that is wicked and rotten in thy sight send thy cleansing fires to devour the vain and idle fancies of our minds and to eat up in its pure flame the filthy and vile habits and desires of our bodies and receive this boy into the healing light of thy redemption. In thy Holy Name, now and forevermore, amen.

The close face, the breath.

—What is it, son? Tell me what it is. Yes. What are you trying to say?

—Please, he whispered. Please, my arm. You're hurting it. Please. You're hurting my arm.

III

For three days he had lain objectified, locked into the silent maelstrom of the casualty. On the third night his eyes were on the window in the ceiling and the blind was up. The moon swam into the window-frame. It filled his eyes with a pale beatitude. He stared at it in a long calm astonishment. It was alive with a benign serenity of light. He felt a smile of recognition breaking across his features. He had awakened to his world again.

—Aha, we came under our own steam, I see. The physiotherapist, brisking in through the agitated doors, there, you moved, it's done. It's you. Casualty. Survivor. Of a kind.

The physiotherapist is talking to you about your groin muscles, but it's nothing personal. She wants them toughened up, who doesn't. Her own must be like steel bands, she looks like a Quaker lady discus thrower. (Comic figures of speech, even – the boy is on the mend. Sad freak.)

— ... to the point where it's able to do the work of a whole leg.

As she lays you on your side, and fits a canvas strap around the fat stump, and you pull with it to lift the weight up and down, and sweat spangles your brow and your testicles slide out through your pyjama flies and you have to smile, just a pinch. Mooncalf.

PART TWO

I

He puts on the short grey coat and the crutches over it. It's a stone-faced day, the city is being picked clean by a wolfish wind. The trees look blanched and calcified. The bus is empty. He doesn't know where to go with the nurse when they meet. The first time they had sat behind a hedge in the park. She made murmurs and grunts as they mumbled each other's faces and mouths, her curious fingers probed his breastbone and vertebrae, lightly touched his upright rock-hard penis, while he roamed over her big body with its wide shoulders and full breasts. The second time they had sat in a cinema, her left arm hanging negligently over his leg. There was no bed he could take her to. There was a bed to sleep in at his parents' house. There would be another one in the flat with Harrison, and a lot of talk and bright clamour. There was no home for his head and his head dragged his disgruntled animal round the streets after it. No place to lay down his head. It was the motif of a hundred cheap songs. He was in transit. There were no familiar shapes moving over the lip of the horizon. He wanted to join the apparitions of the city, the figures who seemed to have no life off the streets, but he found it impossible to lose himself. He was cursed with a voice in the head.

Nobody's moving through the gaunt wind and the traffic except Tosh, today. The smoky warm room of the bus swirls away and he waits at lights for the growl of tyres and gears to pause. He tries to remember the nurse's name. She's engaged to a policeman. It strikes Tosh that she might be experiencing the traditional conflict between the claims of career and those of marriage, and that his demands on her would fit under the first heading. It was a form of physio-therapy. Where would they find to practise it in the drafty vaults of the city today?

He crouches, waiting, on a traffic island, his hips resting against the sign in the middle, the traffic and the wind flowing swiftly round him. He can see across to the wide stone steps. She isn't there yet. He shuffles restlessly up and down in front of the steps. A man passing by stops to say: —Holy God, what have you done to yourself. Was it a motorbike? Them things are lethal.

It slowly dawns on Tosh that the nurse isn't going to come, that he's been stood up. The policeman's claims have won the day. Long after this realisation, he still moves up and down in front of the steps, not knowing where else to go. At last the cold forces him on. He poles his way aimlessly down the streets.

II

The clothes had been a tactile roughhouse at first, when he first slid
them on with awkwardly tremulous hands, sitting on the bed's edge,
his father and the ward sister standing formally by, as they had done
three months before, when the same clothes had been a familiar skin
shed with reluctance and trepidation. Now they nipped his neck,
clammed up high under his arms, heightened the heavy throbbing of
his leg's stump. After three months of limp pyjamas and the shapeless
felt-like green tartan of the dressing-gown, his street clothes seemed
stiff and flamboyant, as assertively symbolic as a flag. They made
him feel puffy and weak.

—Now. Ready for the road? said the ward sister. A few of the
nurses he had known well hovered round the door, less efficiently
businesslike. He offered smiles all round. Polite thanks to the sister.
Clumsy jokes for the nurses. Then he was clanking down the long
corridor with the curved ceiling, his weight landing rhythmically on
an unfamiliar shoe.

His father held open the clear plastic doors into the Outpatients
Dept. and he swung through into *terra nova*. All round him flawed
bodies slumped in rows of chairs, in death's waiting-room, refugees
tossed into a vast terminal by the centrifugal force of the city's life.
The light was dim and the noise softly diffused, the noise of traffic,
with people murmuring quietly or sitting perfectly still, and only the
odd torn-off exclamation or summons offering evidence of human
voices. Eyes flicked up and away again as he passed, registering his
loss but focusing inward on their own, or the fear of it.

He stood at the main door while an attendant opened it. His
father went in front to get the car. He stepped through. Then sun
blared. The sky yawned: there was a harsh rumbling of traffic. His

body swayed a little, he closed his eyes, there were violet shapes, he squeezed the handgrips of the crutches. His father was gesturing. He walked on. The tarmac seemed alarmingly uneven. He was at the car. It was a tiny low box. He detached the left crutch and manoeuvred it into the back seat. Then he turned his back to the car and lowered himself in, his father holding the arm, till he felt his buttocks on the seat, and sweat broke on him and his stump pounded. While his father walked round to the driving seat he detached the other crutch and put it in the back and swung in his leg and closed the door.

The car drove out the gates into the traffic. It all looked filthy. Everything was worn down, shabby, from the footpaths to the railings to the cars and buses covered with thick grime. The sun filmed it all with a cheap brittle light. His eyes hurt, under the unfamiliar weight of clothes sweat pricked him.

When they got to the house his mother opened the kitchen door to him. He looked up at the door, the three steps up seemed grotesquely tall, as tall as his thigh. He wondered if he would topple over backwards and break his spine on the concrete yard. He lunged forward, smiling fixedly, steadied his trembling leg on the first step, balanced carefully for the next, then he was over the threshold. The rooms were shrunken and cluttered with furnishing. He eased himself into the chair beside the radio and record player.

His father had cut out the leg of the striped grey cotton trousers and sewn it up. He was wearing these and a black sweater when he opened the door for Ingrid Robb. She was dressed in a two-piece blue suit, with a handbag and a white umbrella hooked to her wrist.

She dresses like this for job interviews and church with mummy. Also, apparently, for visiting the halt and the deserving poor. She's been fiddling nervously all the way over. She's not very good at comforting the sick. A year or two older and she'll be rushing off for a stiff cocktail after ordeals like this. Mummy's prescription. Paralysed muscles in the face, migraine brows, the whole sad upper-middle crack-up.

—Hello. I thought I'd just pop in. For a bit of a chat. To see if there's anything I can get for you.

Why was I infatuated with you at one time, Ingrid? The broad forehead and the heavy legs. All those ungainly thwartings of my clownish boyish ardour. It must have been a class perversion, the erotic appeal of the frigid bitch in the detached house for the gauche working lad with the jammy mouth.

—Can I come in? Her carefully prepared composure was breaking down under the strain of his intense convalescent stare and the empty air beneath his stump.

He murmured and moved to the side on his crutches to let her pass. She hurried in past him and hovered uncertainly, not knowing whether to close the door and risk offending him or leave him to struggle with it and risk embarrassment. He had a high pitch of awareness of her every gesture of disquiet. He closed the door and nodded towards the living-room, and followed her into it. She stood in the middle of the floor, not knowing where he would want to sit. He nodded towards the sofa, and eased himself into the armchair by the window, beside the radio, where he had sat for the past hundred years or so.

—How are you? She sat with her knees together, ankles crossed, one hand on the handbag, the other on the umbrella.

—I'm alive but not exactly kicking. His mouth spoke this line like a volunteer from the audience reading in for an actor who has met with an accident, he had written it down in all his letters, it was a line from a script which served him now in lieu of conversation, a shoddy anthology of clichés and bad jokes. When he listened to other people talking, they all seemed to be drawing on similar scripts.

She essayed a smile. She wasn't a bad actress. It was at an audition that she first stirred my child's heart. There was something there beyond the elocution and finishing-school self-confidence. There was a life impulse down in there, a tiny vital spark. Only once had she let it burn. When another couple drove with them up to a hilltop near her home, after a party, and they sat in the drunk euphoria in the scent of the car in the rustle of dresses hands and mouths and the sun rose. They were radiant with the inebriation of light, all the humid fragrance of the morning was breathing in their bruised mouths. She was satiated with her awakened senses, her heavy legs were weak as water when she stumbled from the car to her house.

—What's been happening to you, Ingrid?

You let your spark go out. You wore that suit and white gloves when we went together to the TV studios, invited by our producer friend to see it all from the inside. You wriggled your gloved hand away when I took it as we walked along. You've hardened for life now round your ambition.

—I've been finding out about radio and TV jobs. I think I'll be able to get a traineeship. She twiddled the head of her umbrella and stared into the empty grate. The room was empty of sound.

—Are you well off for books? she asked.

—I've been listening to records, he said. Prudence gave me one, I'll play it.

He leaned back towards the record player. He could just touch it with his knuckles. The record almost fell as he placed it across the turntable. He jiggled it round, trying to match its hole to the spindle. He could sense her muscles straining forward to help him and then forcibly pulling back. It was the scene outside the dance hall by the sea at Easter all over again, Monk off looking for pass-outs, the sportive girl observing him sink with dramatised exhaustion against the wall. That had seemed an innocuous dramatisation till the knowledge of isolation crashing over him had been cruelly triggered by it. There were other forces at work now. He knew that Ingrid could never compromise her inhibitions enough to rush over, throw the record aside, babble out the terrors and hopes in her feverish mind, weep anguish at the lingering death of the fantastic promises of adolescence, breathe the poignant sensuous breath she had breathed that daybreak on the hill. She would never do these things. They would all suffer a slow death by strangulation down inside her awkward body.

But some dark impulse, probably cruel, was causing him to give her the opportunity to do them. She started to say Can I help? her voice cracked. He had the record on now, he was straining for the pick-up arm. It was a genuine strain, his hand trembled, but he felt cold as stone. The needle crunched into the middle of the first track. He settled down in the chair again and suddenly wanted to laugh. There was so much in the situation that was ludicrous. The laugh passed across his chest but his mouth stayed shut and grim as though announcing, I have my orders.

—Do you get out – much? Ingrid asked.

—What? He wasn't sure he'd heard her right over the music.

—Do you go out a lot?

—Harold Gams and a friend of his took me out for a drink. In his car. Listen to this next track: it's very tender. Very wistful. I've been playing it a lot.

The music was like cold balm on an interior burn, or spiritual morphine. He watched her as its pores swelled throughout the room's void. She looked as though he'd invited her to listen to a nail scratching a blackboard.

When the first side came to an end he reached back to turn the record over, but she sprang to her feet to forestall him.

—I'll have to be getting on, she said.

—Thanks for calling.

—I was wondering if there was anything I could get you.

—There's not much I need, thanks.

—I thought maybe books. Since everybody's away for the summer. Books for the exams. I could get you those. Lecture notes too.

The exams. Lectures. She sounded almost desperate. He had a vision of her sitting taking lecture notes like a woman knitting mittens for the men at the front.

—Everybody's very kind, he said. It was nice of you to think of that. Exams aren't in my head at the moment. I don't think I could read a book. You know how people who fly gliders talk about searching for thermal turbulence. That's what I seem to be doing mainly.

—Of course. She gave a twisted smile.

—Good-bye Ingrid, he said at the door. He knew he wouldn't see her again except to say hello to in the street.

—I've got it in the other leg, he told Harrison with a tight voice. Harrison's haggard pallor had not noticeably diminished during the summer abroad: now his face was hardening with tension.

—It couldn't happen, he said.

Tosh, hawk-like, saw the flicker of fearful doubt which belied this.

—That's what I told myself when the pain started. I kept saying it and it kept getting sorer. It's the same pain in the same place.

—It's a psychosomatic reaction, said Harrison. You must be unconsciously afraid of it happening again and your body's responding to the fear. It's a sort of sympathetic pain.

—That's what I thought – until it started to swell.

Harrison pulled sharply on his cigarette and blew the smoke out equally sharply. —Is it swelled much?

—About the same as before.

Tosh closed his eyes. The fear that he felt now was the old kind, not the icy quietude of the night before the amputation, but the gutchurning kind which made him want to bite into his fingers, to whimper like a child, to be fed morphine, somehow to lose himself and the intolerable hours ahead of him.

—Have you talked to anybody else about it? said Harrison.

—I told the family minister. He's a pathetic clown of a man but he arrived at a time when I had to tell somebody. He was the only one available. I would have blabbed it out to a deaf-mute if one had appeared that particular day. There's nobody else knows. I don't want to mention it to the family – until it's absolutely certain.

—You haven't been up to the hospital yet?

—No. I've been waiting for you to show up. I want you to come up with me.

—Okay, when?

—Now.

—Fine.

Harrison stood up and gave a wry and mirthless laugh of reassurance.

—They wouldn't do it on you, he said. The heavens wouldn't shit on you twice in the same place. They're subtler than that.

—There isn't anything subtler than that, said Tosh.

He went through to his mother in the kitchen.

—We're going out for a few hours, he said.

—You'll watch yourself in the traffic, won't you?

—I'll keep an eye on him, Harrison called.

In the bus Harrison talked about his summer. Tosh was glad of the voice but barely listened. He was talking over in his head the meaning of these new pitiless emotional waters into which he had sailed. One element of his fear was straightforward enough: his resources were not capable of carrying him back through the furnace out of which he had just emerged. If this new obscene swelling meant what the first one had, he would break down, the machinery would gnarl up and grind into splinters. But there was something worse. He was in terror now, for the first time, of his consciousness. For three days he had felt the controls slithering, a ground-swell of hysterical irrationality rising up to engulf him. Now he knew that this was the thing he feared most. That was why Prudence's compulsive obsessiveness, his mother's long shrill quarrel with her life, even Harrison's surly barracking, had maddened him and at the same time provoked a stolid refusal to respond. He had shunned their claims on him, had refused to entertain claims, because their goaded unrestrainable hearts had clawed at the passions in his own, and he was afraid to acknowledge or unleash them. He was emotionally as well as physically halt. He had been an emotional coward, and the feelings he had shrunk most sharply away from were his own because their power appalled him. Now they were rising up to dominate him. He had felt contempt for his mother's hypochondria and ugly outbursts of howling tear-stained recrimination, of Prudence's abject lack of restraint; instead of meeting their feelings with feelings of his own, he had locked himself into a stony face. There was to be no floating free in his own head. He would only be able to float free through other people. He didn't know whether that was possible any longer.

In the hospital outpatients department he asked to see the surgeon. They sat for a few minutes amidst the broken rank of stricken people, Harrison's voice constricting more and more under the strain. A physiotherapist appeared and said she had been instructed to x-ray the leg. She was puzzled that his whole leg was the one specified. He showed her the swelling under the knee and she sat him on a table under the great umbrella of equipment. He hadn't been sure at first about the swelling, there was no left leg with which to compare it. Then he had become surer and surer till he was finally convinced that he could detect an increase in the swelling overnight. The physiotherapist finished and told him to return to outpatients and the surgeon would send for him when the x-rays were ready.

—I haven't felt changed, he told Harrison as they sat hunched nervously in the moulded plastic seats. I'd expected to find it was all radically different when I left this place.

—You don't seem much changed. Just convalescent. When we find the flat you'll be able to live just like before it all happened.

—That's what the surgeon said the night before it. That's not true either, though. The only reason I don't feel the changes is because I was so undefined before. I was just adrift, and I'm still adrift. The changes are going on down deep somewhere. I was scared even before this new pain started.

They watched the perspex doors to the wards as they talked, swishing to and fro continually in the heavy everyday traffic of sickness and death.

—Any word of the artificial leg? said Harrison.

—They fit you up with a crude kind of effort at first called a pylon limb. Until you can walk. Then they give you the life-sized flesh-coloured number.

—With hairs and a bunion.

—And gear levers under the knee-cap.

He saw a nurse coming towards them.

—But they won't measure me up for it until the swelling in the stump has diminished.

He stood up as he spoke, and moved towards the nurse on his crutches. She led him up to the ward. In the treatment room opposite his side ward, the surgeon was waiting for him.

—The other leg's giving you bother? he murmured.

—There's the same pain and the same swelling in the same place.

Tosh felt wild. If the surgeon had bad news this time, there wouldn't be any phlegmatic decent-chap behaviour, he would do violence.

—What's the likelihood? he asked and his voice shook.

—The chances against it are vast, said the surgeon, examining the knee. Don't forget that this leg is taking all the strain now, after being out of commission for three months. There's every chance of muscular pain.

—I've had that, said Tosh brusquely. I know what that's like. This is different. It's exactly like the other leg.

The surgeon moved away and picked up the x-rays.

—Well there's nothing here that I can see, he said. There's nothing at all wrong with your leg. So I'd advise you to go back home and forget all about it.

He left. Tosh sat on the table, his trouser leg pulled up, and felt suddenly sick and foolish. He pushed the trouser leg slowly down and made his way back. Harrison looked like the illest person in the Outpatients Department.

—He says there's nothing there, said Tosh.

They went and had a drink. Harrison was flown with relief.

—You can get drunk quicker now, he said. The blood doesn't have as far to travel, right?

—People are shocked enough at the sight of me. If they saw me humping along the footpath drunk they'd run screaming through the streets.

Entering was like a beggars' burlesque of royalty. Little bald men, a vivid tracery of fine red veins on their noses and cheek-bones, stood about in the hallway behind the smudged glass and tarnished brass of the doors. As Tosh swung slowly up on his crutches, two of them, their dark blue livery misshapen on their bodies like arthritic fingers, sprang to the doors and whipped them solemnly open.

He proceeded majestically through to the middle of the dusty hall, and a third attendant stepped forward out of the gloom.

—Is it limbs, sir? he asked respectfully.

Tosh nodded.

—Third floor. There's the lift there.

—This way, sir. It was the voice of yet another attendant, calling from the dark corner where a cage door clearly gave access to a lift.

The lift had a single bare bulb screwed to the ceiling and all the symptoms of asthma. When the third floor was gained, the lift-man threw the brass lever back and forth, the lift shuddering up and down till its floor was level with the floor outside. Then he threw back the metal door with an impressive clang and flourish.

—Have you been here before sir, do you know where to go?

—No, said Tosh.

—Just follow that corridor till you see the waiting-room. There's a sign outside it. The wee girl in there will look after you.

Tosh launched himself down the corridor. There was a door marked Eye Fitting, then one marked Limb Workshop. Coming towards him were two white-coated figures, leading by the hand between them a child of five or six. The child had a strap over his shoulder and a waist belt holding on what looked like metal callipers on his right leg, except that there was no leg. The metal frame terminated in a punt-shaped block of wood instead of a foot. The child was bawling and the two men murmuring to him in a kindly way: they continued murmuring as they nodded to Tosh in passing.

Ahead there was another corridor joining from the left. At the junction a large bunch of artificial legs were stacked upright. Some were a maidenly pink and others had the look of a synthetic sun-tan. He had seen photographs of artificial legs stacked just like them at Auschwitz and Belsen, along with everything else that could be removed from the bodies of gassed Jews. It had been somehow more disturbing than even the shaven, spindly body-spooks. Why so? A kind of human refuse. Detritus of bottles and tin cans in the white sand of a desert.

On his right he saw the waiting-room and swung into it. It was small and narrow, dingy armchairs along each side with half a dozen men in them. At the end, under a window, in front of a radiator, facing him, in a wheelchair, there sat half a man. He had a large gnarled head. He looked at least a hundred years old. His body came to an end just below his buttocks. In the side wall, near to this man, there was a window hatch with a handwritten sign ENQUIRIES jutting out. Tosh picked his way towards this between the parallel lines of feet.

A woman appeared at the window hatch after he had knocked on it. She took his name and told him to sit down. He chose the nearest end chair, its seat and back greasily dark with use, a small round table beside it strewn with torn pages of aged women's magazines. Nobody was talking in the room. He scanned the line of feet opposite. One foot of each pair sat cocked on its heel at an odd angle; in two cases, a shiny brown patch of leg visible above the top of the sock contrasted oddly with the hairy whiteness of the corresponding patch alongside it. By these signs shall we be known. Tosh raised his eyes discreetly and scrutinised the faces: a young red-haired country boy, a heavy-set man with hair in his nostrils, a thin old man with violet strings of veins across the backs of his hands. It had not occurred to him till now that he was a member of a freemasonry. A novice arrived for initiation.

A little man in a sleeveless Fair Isle pullover and horn-rimmed glasses erupted suddenly into the room, dipping up and down as he walked on a stiff left leg.

—Shannon, Haslitt! he announced loudly as he swept up to the window hatch, planted some forms down on its ledge and picked up two others. Two of the figures in the chairs got themselves upright in a gingerly manner, one of them creaking loudly.

—You're Mr. Tosh? said the stiff-legged man.

—Yes.

—The doctor'll see to you in a minute, Mr. Tosh. Are you doing all right Mr. Weeks? he shouted at the legless ancient trunk in the wheelchair.

—Wha's that?

—I'll wheel you down for a cup of tea in a minute.

—Eh?

But the stiff-legged man had already left at full tilt, followed by the two he had summoned. He was clearly the kind of disabled person who was talked about admiringly by his able-bodied acquaintances in terms like He walks me off my feet, nothing tires him, he always has a cheerful word for you; whilst they struggled to suppress their private dislike of him as an officious, overbearing, self-important boor.

Fifteen minutes later he appeared again to summon Tosh. By the time Tosh had got to the door, the stiff-legged man was out of sight; but his voice echoed up the long corridor calling —This way! Following the voice, Tosh arrived at a door into an ante-room and almost collided with the stiff-legged man coming out again, who said breezily:

—We'll have to get you motorised crutches. On through here.

He threw open an inner door, proclaimed —Mr. Tosh, doctor! and left as soon as Tosh had passed the threshold.

The doctor pushed awkwardly round in his chair. He was old, tired-looking, his shoulder curved almost into a hunchback. On his desk there was nothing except, in one corner, fifty or so loose cigarettes piled up like logs, and a large tin ash-tray.

—Sit down there, he said almost inaudibly, motioning to an examination bed built into the wall by his desk. —Let down your trousers please.

As Tosh unloosed his trousers, the doctor lifted a cigarette with long graceful fingers from the pile and lit it with the butt of the one in his mouth. Then he stubbed out the butt very slowly, almost negligently. The bandage fell off the stump with the sewn-up trouser leg. With the fresh cigarette smoking in the corner of his mouth, the doctor picked it up, placed it on the desk, and leaned forward intently studying the stump. He pressed it with his long fingers, and touched the back of his hand to its tip. He grunted, turned back to the desk, produced a folder and wrote in it. Then he took the pin from the bandage and slowly started to roll it up. Through all this Tosh watched, slightly mesmerised by the painstaking aged slowness of the doctor's every movement. Not a gesture was either wasted or fumbled. Everything was performed in a precise slow motion. By the time the bandage was fully rolled up, the cigarette had almost burned away. Again, a fresh one was drawn carefully from the stockpile and lit with slightly trembling fingers.

—After you've been measured come back here and I'll put the bandage on again. You can pull up your trousers and wait next door. Mr. Armstrong'll take care of you.

Tosh moved into the adjacent room. After a few minutes, one of the two white-coated men whom he had seen leading the child by the hand appeared.

—Would you come this way, please. Mr. Tosh, isn't it?

The man was middle-aged, wiry dark hair dusted with grey. He walked slowly a pace or two in front of Tosh, preceding him along the corridor and into a large bare room, and motioning him into a chair.

—If you sit there I'll be with you in two shakes. You can put your other leg on again Peter.

This last was addressed to a thin boy of about seventeen who was seated on a throne-like chair on a dais against the wall. The chair had hand-rails built round it, the front one hinging outwards. The boy was in his underpants and his right leg ended in mid-calf. Tosh stared at the uneven inflamed stump with incredulous fascination. It was the first naked one apart from his own which he'd seen. The existence of the knee made it somehow more grotesque, made it even harder for the thwarted eye to accept the empty space beneath. The boy was pulling a long woollen sausage-shaped garment out of the tin leg, which leant against the dais, clothed in a shoe and sock and trousers, with an unnerving sentient human existence.

—One tip, Peter, said the limb-fitter. Don't leave your stump socks in the leg when you take it off. Always take the sock out and fold it. It'll last twice as long and it'll be more comfortable.

The boy pulled the sock over his stump and inserted it into the tin leg without replying. Then he fastened the belt round his hips, pulled up his trousers and put the shoe on his left foot. Then he pushed the hinged hand-rail open and stepped down off the dais.

—You should hear from us in a month or two, said the limb-fitter.

The boy unhooked an overcoat from the wall and put it on. Tosh watched as he walked out. The limp was negligible. But the boy had a knee.

—Now, Mr. Tosh. Just throw your coat off and climb up to the chair. Here, I'll give you a hand. That's you. I want to get all your vital statistics. Take off your shoe, sock and trousers, if you will.

Tosh propped his crutches against the wall and sat down in the big chair. As he stripped, he scrutinised the heavily detailed form which the limb-fitter was spreading at the front of the dais.

—What height are you?

—Five-eleven, said Tosh. The limb-fitter wrote it down.

—Do you happen to know your weight?

—Well – not now. Not without the leg.

—Never worry, you can step on to the scales at the end. Now if you'll stand upright we'll get the measurements on this stump. Keep your back straight and head up. Good. Now. You're letting the stump sag a bit which is natural. But I want you to even it up.

The limb-fitter, his eyes on a level with Tosh's thighs, cupped his hands round Tosh's loins and put his thumbs on the twin front bumps of his hip bones, then leaned back, estimating the straightness of the line between them.

—Good. Try and keep like that.

He lifted on to the dais a contraption like a piano stool, placed it under the stump and turned the round piece of wood on its long screw till Tosh felt it graze the bottom of his stump. Then he removed it and looped a tape-measure round the top of the stump, sliding it up into the groin. He repeated this several times before recording a measurement, and then did the same a little way down the stump and so on to the bottom.

—What do you do with yourself, are you a student? he asked as he worked.

—That's right.

—You fellows have the brave times.

He chuckled a little to himself.

—I was just thinking of the last student Rag Day. Somehow or other a crowd of them managed to get themselves up in this place. They came charging round the corner of the corridor there, shaking their collecting boxes and yelling blue murder.

He stopped measuring for a moment to step back and mime the incident.

—There was limbs lying about the place and a double amp case sitting outside the waiting-room. By God you never saw a quicker change! They stopped dead in their tracks, turned round and walked back out without so much as a squeak.

He shook his head, relishing the memory, and Tosh smiled back. The limb-fitter turned a page of the form.

—I want to get the details of your good leg now. He began measuring again.

—Is a double amp a person with both legs off? asked Tosh.

—Two limbs. Can you support yourself on your arms a minute, till I slide this under your foot? That's it.

He carefully traced with a pencil the outline of the foot onto a blank page of the form.

—That boy that was here before you, he said. You should see his brother. Amazing. They were both in a bad car accident. The brother lost both his legs and an arm. A young fellow, just about your own age. It's the worst case I've seen. But he's as wild as ever. He's driving again, he's got a job in a bank. Of course he was lucky in a way, they were able to save a knee and his elbow.

He straightened up and put the tape-measure in his pocket.

—You can dress yourself again now, that's you finished.

—I suppose you meet with a lot of incredible cases in here.

The limb-fitter smiled at him.

—You'll meet with plenty yourself, he said.

Tosh tied his shoe-lace. I'm not a visitor here, I'm a new inmate. I'm a case myself. I'm badged for life.

—Did the doctor want to see you again?

—He told me to go back to him to be bandaged again.

—Oh aye, you could do with that, right enough. The stump's still puffed up a bit. I've allowed for a bit more shrinkage in the measurements.

Tosh put on his coat.

—What kind of thing will I be getting?

—We'll be starting you off on what's called a pylon limb. It's a simple metal framework with a curved bit of wood on the bottom. It's just to help you get your balance and get you used to walking. Then we'll make you a proper articulated leg.

—How long will I be using the pylon leg?

—Two or three months.

Tosh fitted his crutches. The limb-fitter led him back to the doctor's office, knocked, and ushered him in.

—Thanks a lot, said Tosh.

—We'll be in touch when your pylon limb's ready to be fitted.

The doctor sat hunched at his desk as before, smoking his way through the white pyramid of cigarettes. With an unhurried deliberation he wound the bandage in layers round the stump and pinned it.

It was still in place, firm and neat, five days later, when Tosh finally had to remove it to be washed.

Something fell through with regard to the flat, some misunderstanding was germinated in the serpentine processes of Harrison's dealings with other people, and they were left in the lurch a few days before term started, with all the available housing long since taken.

—I've been busy moving mountains, the matronly Housing Officer told them, rather coldly. —You're to go and see a Mr. McKenzie at this address right away. He thinks he might have a place ready for you in a week or two. I told him there were... special difficulties. He's a sort of health doctor and he sees how you're placed. I gather he has a house being converted at the moment, anyway he'll tell you about it himself.

There was a door-plate saying Naturopath.

—He must have made that word up, said Tosh.

—I think I've seen it in magazine ads.

They were shown into a room with tall lamps like a photographer's studio but with an examination bed built along one wall. After a while a door opened and a man with a fuzz of grey hair, with heavy black eyebrows accentuating a gaze that was meant to rivet, confronted them.

—I'm completely familiar with the details of your case, he announced, pointing at Tosh. —You're not alone. There've been seven cases of malignancy amongst young people – seven! – during the past few months in this city. Four of them are dead, thanks to the miracles of modern science.

He turned dramatically on his heel back into the office.

—Come in, sit down! he shouted over his shoulder.

They sat on a black leather sofa to the side of his desk. He scrutinised them with his bright stare, leaning back in his swivel chair.

—Mrs. Sloan said you might have... began Harrison.

—Carving bodies up, they're very good at that. After they've pumped a lot of synthetic poison into you. That's when people come to me, when the worst has been done, when there's nobody else to turn to. It's far too late then, of course. They refuse to go to the cause, the root cause that's staring them in the face.

He leaned forward, eyes boring into Tosh.

—Tell me this. Do you eat a lot of fries?

The question hung for a few moments suspended in incredulous silence.

—Fries? No, not that many. No more than anybody else, anyway.

—It's a dietary matter. It all comes back to diet, that stands to reason. Everything you put into your body has its consequences, surely you can see that.

He leaned back again.

—You probably know the case of that boy of nineteen, the long-jumper.

Tosh shook his head.

—Tragic case, a boy with a brilliant athletic career ahead of him. Died just last month. I've tried, I've done what I can. They wouldn't even accept my recommendations on their own hospital diet. It's a scandal.

His face darkened.

—Any aches and pains since you got out of hospital?

—He's okay, said Harrison. He's fine.

—I've two or three houses you could have had a flat in, very nice. If you'd come four or five weeks ago. You've left it far too late.

—You don't have anything, then? asked Tosh.

—Mrs. Sloan assured us... began Harrison testily.

—I've a house in the process of conversion. You'll need some-where close to the university with that? He gestured at Tosh.

—Yes. Close.

—I suppose they'll be fitting you out with a prosthesis soon, though.

—It'll be a month or two yet.

—That's where the money goes, you see. Prevention never occurs to them. They're always announcing some new miracle drug but how many diseases have they succeeded in curing, let alone eliminating? Panaceas and nostrums, quackery, that's what it all amounts to. Did they try to tell you the cause of your tumour?

—They said they didn't yet know the causes.

—By God they're making precious little effort to redeem their ignorance.

He looked slowly from Tosh to Harrison and back as if inviting them to concur.

—This flat wasn't to be occupied till after Christmas but I'm prepared to bend a point in this instance. The bathroom isn't in yet.

—No bathroom at all? asked Harrison.

—There's one upstairs. You've the right to use it, the upstairs flat isn't self-contained. There's girls in it. They'll need to come through occasionally to get at their coal in the yard.

—How about furniture?

—I've got two divan beds ordered, they should be in by the end of the week. The rest will come in due course. I can do no more than that. You'll have to put up with the workmen till Christmas.

He gave them the address and a key. They stood up.

—There's precious little profit in being a landlord these days, he said. I don't normally have students as tenants. The girls are nurses, very well-behaved and punctual with the rent. I've had more than enough trouble in the past, believe you me. So long as there are no complaints from neighbours and no destruction of furniture I won't bother you. The rent is due on the first day of each month.

He accompanied them to the front door.

—There's two excellent vegetarian restaurants down the town, he said to Tosh. Eat sensibly and you'll have very little to worry about.

At last they were in the street and walking away.

—To hell with that, said Tosh.

—We've no choice, we'll have to take it. We can look at it anyway.

—Give us a cigarette.

Magazine of a girls' private school, pages of gangly poems and stories, the School Play, Cercle Français, the sports teams in regimented photographs. News of Last Year's Sixth. Alphabetical listing of the Old Girls Association. One hockey photograph. One face.

You want to write a letter to her. One girl's face, caught by chance in a team photograph. You're demented enough to do that. She can't be older than seventeen. Back Row L to R: H. Adamson J. L. Prentice R. Vickers (Capt.) T. H. Jamison H. Lucas. H: Helen, perhaps. Hazel. Lucas.

Where did it come from? My mother brought it in from somewhere. She always brings in something. There might be some reading for you in that, son.

Golden curls. Unconscious sexual grace. But it's the expression. Mystery of the young gaze.

You would do that, you're heart-sick enough. You've always done those foolish goaded things, even when you were meant to be a child. You stayed on the bus coming home from school because a girl was upstairs. You got off when she did and followed her on to another bus. You stayed on till she got off again, almost at the terminus. You followed her home and walked three times past her gate. Then you took the two slow buses home. You phoned them up, affecting disguised voices. You stood bated for hours, to watch them pass by.

Because you see them either as harpies or Beatrices; first as a Beatrice, then as a harpy. Your masculine bequest, that. It has to end. You turn to a woman expecting God incarnate, you're hot for godhead more than maidenhead, it has to end.

You want to write to her. You'll do it, you damned fool, you're ravenous enough for mystery. Something to do, something to feel.

Narcissism, the mind of a pubescent schoolboy mooning in his room, sending foolish valentines. It's throwing out a forlorn anchor. Anything you like. I'm drowning in my own breath, devouring the oxygen in this sealed airless box. There's nobody. I'm in touch with nobody.

You invent. You want to invent this nymphet madonna. You need to fuel your fantasies. You've no resources to grapple the actual world.

She still holds you. Dew on a flower-bud gazing at you. It sets you aching restlessly for some chimera of the heart.

Anything you like. I'm going to write.

It was most kind of you to write me a letter, after seeing me in our school mag. Well, I didn't think the photograph was up to much myself although very glad you liked it. In reply to what you asked about here, this is a school of 530 girls though most are boarders like me some are day pupils. The boarders come from all over the country and have on the whole a better time, at least I think so! It's not too bad, though some teachers are fussy. (Like Miss Hawkins!) (She's the head). They're always on about wearing earrings etc. It's so small-minded but others are good fun especially Miss Burns the games mistress (see photo). Hope you will write again soon. Bye for now, Hetty Lucas.

Harold Gams at the door one evening, suited and tied, a fair-haired privileged-looking chap behind him.

—Drinks on me and this offer is unrepeatable, so get your coat. By the way this is Peter Anderson.

Harold was slightly more fraught than normal. Tosh detached a hand from the right crutch and shook the proffered hand of the blond friend. Lager in the lounge bar. Sports talk and a little current affairs.

—Thanks Harold but it's hardly worth all the trouble. Another night, maybe.

—On with the coat and no more excuses.

—I don't think I'll bother.

—All right, you'll just have to come coatless.

Harold grabbing him roughly by the arm, over-excited with nerves. The friend was looking uncomfortable. —If he really doesn't... he started to say to Harold, but Tosh had already succumbed, smiling ruefully, if only to resolve the situation.

Harold fussed around him as he eased into the car. Then they were driving to a pub outside the city, with horse brasses and men discussing golf while their wives deplored their children's strange ways.

Tosh had not lost yet the patina of convalescence. The world speeding round him was one to treat in gingerly fashion, thinking out your every movement, preparing it slowly and methodically. Like a traveller freshly awake in a foreign household full of welcoming strangers, he felt conspicuous, vulnerable in his weakness, wary of blunders. As Harold Gams and his friend talked, Tosh observed this alien landscape, slipping in the odd word to keep as unobtrusive as possible.

While Harold was locking the parked car, a small boy approached Tosh, who was leaning on his crutches.

—Where's your leg? he said, amazed.

—It fell off down the road there.

—It didn't not.

—I'm telling you.

—You've got it tucked up some way.

The boy walked around Tosh, incredulously; then he reached out his hand and touched the stump with his finger-tips as though it were some unprecedented animal.

—Okay, clear off, said Harold, coming up, stiff with embarrassment.

—What happened it? said the boy.

—It just fell right off and we left it up the road there, said Tosh.

—It couldn't of.

—Beat it, said Harold, endeavouring to lead Tosh towards the pub. But the boy followed alongside.

—Will it not grow again?

—No, said Tosh. It'll just stay like this.

Harold pushed the child roughly out of the way and held open the pub door.

—It's just lying beside the road? said the child.

—Certainly, said Tosh. But you needn't bother looking for it at this time of the night.

In the pub they drank three lagers each and talked sports and politics. When they had dropped him back home again, Tosh felt fairly certain that they were as relieved as he that the evening was over.

You must have a place to land and rest. You must have a way to break free of this thrall which is losing you your life.

Harrison had arranged for free tickets for the next formal dance. In return they would provide entertainment during the intermission. They sat in the flat in borrowed evening dress, drinking from small bottles of brandy, Harrison restlessly organising in his nervy, uninflected voice:

—You know what Alice Cook's like. Maybe I should handle her. On the other hand Sinéad might be a drag on you. Do you know her at all? She seems heavily Catholic, but sometimes they're truly volcanic. Anyway, we'll play it by ear. Make sure you've got the words of the songs. I've got it set up for you to borrow a guitar from the band. So we don't need to hump yours over there.

The girls arrived. There was a lot of loud edgy talk, over drinks. Then they all walked to the dance through an autumnal twilight, remorse and wild longing almost palpable in the cool auburn atmosphere full of excited birds. A burst of hot scented air came from the hall, along with the cavernous crashing of the band.

Tosh sat in the balcony drinking from the bottle, his arm around Sinéad. There was something jogging him. He turned, it was an attendant jabbing at the damned pylon leg, telling him that drinking outside the bar area was not allowed. He wondered for how long the attendant had been tapping his leg.

They danced. She spun, he caught her, they swayed and shuffled on one spot. She was breathless, her eyes bright and wide.

At the intermission he clambered on to the stage with Harrison and set up a music stand for the words of his comic songs. He'd forgotten his glasses, Harrison had to hold the words a few inches in front of his nose. Even then he missed many of them, making a nonsense of the songs. Always before a spring in him had wound up for occasions like this, providing co-ordination and resilience to carry it off, no matter how drunk or ill-prepared. The spring was broken, he didn't care. The dancers catcalled, pennies began to shower on to the stage. He was anaesthetised, it was happening to his animal puppet, not to him.

Beside him Harrison ran through their skits and songs, his face set tight in its hard pallor. Then a pianist and drummer came on and Tosh joined them, sitting with his back to the audience which had built up to a barrage of jeering. They ran through three or four numbers, Tosh playing to his own mind, occasionally aware that the piano and drums were out of co-ordination. By the time the band filtered on again, he had forgotten that he was sitting on a stage at all.

At the end of the dance they lurched home hugging and collapsed into chairs in the living-room.

—Look at him, said Harrison. He doesn't look bad for a man in a borrowed suit.

—Maybe he's a saint, said Alice Cook.

He kissed Sinéad in an armchair, her breathing squally, the low-cut satin dress sliding easily off her fleshy breasts. When he caressed them, her head twisted on his shoulder, her breath quickening to gasps and little cries. He observed her out of a dead calm. Ecstasy was padlocked into self, like suffering. The sobbing breaths, the mouth biting at air, convulsed torso, what was it all but an anguish to burst the lock that would never give way. His hand slid down her stomach and she clutched at him with hardening groans. She was drowning under his hand, fighting towards an articulate cry. Lost to him, to the world.

Harrison and Alice Cook melted away to the next room. He took Sinéad by the hand to the bed, her face arrested in a swollen drowse. She sank down gathering him into her and folding her face and closing eyes into his shoulder. He kissed the lids and the burning cheeks and pulled the long liquid skirts up over her knees. When his hand moved up between her thighs the inarticulate storm broke out again and his fingers in the mound of coarse hair and moist opening galvanised her whole body till it was wrenched over on its side and back again, her head flung backwards and forwards, lifting and dropping again. He watched it all in a dead calm. Now should be the moment to slide into her and abandon himself to the rough sea. She was fumbling with him, tugging to release the hardened shaft to feed it into her turbulent belly. Not helping her, he worked insistently with his fingers till she abandoned him with a cry and gave herself up to the waves breaking across her. He looked on till the spasms diminished and then withdrew his hand. For the first time an emotion crept over him, a faint flush of remorse.

—Come on, he said. We'll get into bed.

—Why? she said faintly. It's all right.

He paused irresolutely, a hand on the zip at the back of her dress. She hugged him and nuzzled his face. She didn't object to his voyeuristic detachment, then. Maybe preferred it. To a frenzied mutuality of solitudes. She was talking, warm chatty gossip of intimacy. She was happy, released, she would be able to fashion out of the evening any meaning or memory she wanted most to adopt.

He lay with his mouth against her forehead, the flow of her voice cocooning them, and stared into the dark wall. So it was till the other two made warning returning noises, and they slid their legs off the bed and switched on the light and sat wincing sleepily in the bright glare.

After the two girls had gone, Harrison turned to him with an overstrung energy in his voice.

—Well, did you score?

—Eh?

—You got it all right? I was a bit worried – with the leg – I thought it might give you problems. Might be difficult.

Tosh looked at him faintly astonished.

—It never crossed my mind.

—You're okay then?

—Certainly. Good God. Tosh laughed. There was madness in all of it. Harrison was clapping him heartily on the shoulder with a rough masculine guffaw.

—You got one up on me, you prick. Cook was in her moons, wouldn't let me touch her.

Cora called, to rehabilitate you. She had the right idea, up to a point. Others offered books and concern, or a drive in the country. She offered her warm flesh, up to a point. First you were too reluctant, then you were too ardent.

It seemed a long time before that he'd given up on Cora, but she'd been to the hospital several times, she was working in social welfare now, that was the reason for the reluctance, she carried on a cheerful serene intercourse with the world at large. Her earthiness was unconscious, her progress down the road of motherhood and respectable affluence steadfast and not to be impeded.

There was no forgetting their first encounter. It had been the end of a dance, swollen heavy with shadows and the accumulated spoor of the evening. He had seen her come in with a friend, her head was a cluster of blonde curls and she had an aura of physical unconcern, slightly overweight and dressed without guile. In the midst of such ruthless calculation, he homed in on her. She laughed a lot. She was relaxed with herself. And as they mooned around the floor, she held his left hand in such a way that the tip of the thumb brushed back and forward, back and forward across the nipple of her right breast. It was a piece of absent-minded sensuality that inflamed and delighted him more than any provocative deliberation ever could. He clowned and capered for her and was ready to throw in his lot with her, surrender any plans or principles in return for a lifetime of such blithe unawareness. But she was promised to a pilot and was only filling in the time till he got his wings and could marry her. Tosh found this situation hilarious. He treasured Cora for her inability to take him seriously. For a while he thought that he might be edging the pilot out of the picture, but their marital union became clearly more ineluctable and Tosh finally stopped seeing a lot of Cora, with the same equanimity that had governed their friendship from the first night at the dance.

She came in her car to inveigle him off to the pictures.

—Too much awkward struggling, he said. But without apparent effort she had him in the car in coat and scarf. She chided all of his weak complaints.

—Actually, I really wanted to go pony trekking, he said when they were finally seated in the cinema. She smiled up into his face, her eyes swimming with laughter, and closed her loosely smiling mouth on his, the dark kiss entering his blood like alcohol. Then she thrust her head into his neck, embracing him loosely, and they spent the film joking and nuzzling like youngsters on a first date.

By the time she had him home again, he felt more alive than he had since leaving the hospital. She called often after that. In her loose summer cotton dresses and bare white legs she had an almost slatternly look that made him long to be naked with her in the sun, to lose the stasis and morbidity of his life in the strenuous joyful benediction of love play (the joyful tumult of sweat and flesh). However, as he remarked in a letter to Harrison, when making a pass involves struggling on to your foot, clamping a pair of crutches to your forearms, humping across the room, lowering yourself carefully down on the sofa beside the woman, detaching the crutches and putting them aside, you'll understand that cool suave sexuality is beyond me. She would always come to him, establishing an easy physical bond as soon as she arrived, settling down on the ground in front of his chair, arms spread across his lap. Then he would kiss and caress her.

But these preliminaries were all she would allow him. As in their original period of intimacy, the shadow of the pilot fell between them. Tosh was bemused, arrested in the middle of an erotic overture, by Cora's admission that the pilot had laid down what she might and might not do in her relations with Tosh.

Her ministrations were spontaneous and sincere — but, equally, they were professional and that rankled with Tosh when she wasn't there and his mind would work things over with carnivorous thoroughness. She loved him, she was a welfare officer, she loved all the lame ducks within her discernment, in a cheerful unconsidered way. It wasn't enough. He was grateful to her.

She stopped coming round after he moved into the flat with Harrison.

Armstrong came in, carrying the pylon limb. It looked like some odd fitment off an early aeroplane, with its cylindrical top and the thick metal struts leading down to the heavy crescent of wood. A brown label was tied on it.

—I'll be back in a minute to fit this on you, said the limb-fitter. Just slip your coat and trousers off.

Tosh looked at the label. It had his name on it and the date, and a long number. It's a new bit of you. Identify with it.

—I was at a hospital charity affair one time, the minister was saying, and these two chaps in wheelchairs were comparing notes. One of them had been wounded very badly in the thighs during the war, and his legs were more or less paralysed. And you'll never guess what my name is, he says to the other fellow. It's Shanks. You see? So the other one laughs a bit and says, that's nothing. I stepped right on top of a exposed electric cable, and what d'you think I'm called? Foot! Well, gentlemen, said I, I'm pleased to meet you both. I'm the Reverend Harry Legge. And with that I pulled up the trouser flap and gave the limb a good sound rap. Well, they laughed till there was tears in their eyes. It was a good one.

—Oh, that was a quare gag all right, said the welder, clearing his throat uneasily. Foot and Legge. Right enough, it makes you think.

—I remember one time during the war I was in an air raid shelter, resumed the Reverend Harry Legge.

He was a small squat figure in dog collar and silver-rimmed spectacles, dwarfed by the unwieldy bulk of the welder who sat in the next chair, in his shapeless double-breasted suit, his hair cropped high above the big gnarled ears and crudely shaved on the beefy neck in long strips that looked like burn marks. Some distance from him sat a distinguished-looking family doctor, in white shirt and collegiate tie, reading *The Times*. At the end of the shallow semi-circle of chairs sat an ancient farmer, grizzled and toothless. Tosh was fascinated by how their appearances from the waist up, including his own, proclaimed an almost caricatured identity: whilst from the waist down, they were equally trouserless, each with one whole white and hairy leg and one longer or shorter stump of its fellow. Of course the farmer's soiled long johns tell a story. And the doctor's sock suspenders and hand-made brown brogue. Still. We make a right spectacle. For cartoonists of the human condition.

The Reverend Legge was interrupted in mid-anecdote by a limb-fitter coming in with the welder's battered tin leg under his arm.

—What in the name of God have you been doing to this? he asked.

The welder shifted uncomfortably in the small chair and attempted a hoarse ingratiating laugh.

—It just went from under me, you see, he said. Threw me on my back. Just like that. In the middle of the shop floor, you follow me? So anyway, there I am flat out on my back and I can't get up. So... it was the knee, you see. Gone for a burton. So all the lads was standing round me, you know? And one of the wee apprentices looks at the leg and says that there's a riveting job, so it is. So one of the riveters gets his gear over. He done a right good job, mind you.

The welder laughed again, turning to the Reverend Legge for concurrence in the jest, but the minister was maintaining a front of genial oblivion.

—How long ago was this? asked the limb-fitter.

—Well now, wait till we see, said the welder, greatly abashed by this question. —It would probably be a matter of a few months anyway.

—You've been walking round on this for several months?

—He done a really good job, you know? Like, it did me rightly up till yesterday evening.

—It's scrap, said the limb-fitter simply. He looked steadily at the welder for a few moments, then he shook his head and smiled slightly.

—You're a desperate man, what are we going to do with you?

The welder laughed sheepishly, saying: —It was a lovely job of riveting, I was up and about again in a matter of minutes.

—We can fix your spare leg up as a temporary measure, but this here's scrap. We'll have to make you a new limb.

The welder laughed awkwardly again, saying something unintelligible.

—It'll take the boys a couple of hours to patch up your spare limb, so there's nothing for it but to wait. I'll take your measurements before you go.

The limb-fitter left and there was a moment's strained silence.

—It was the best laugh, said the welder. There's me sitting up in the middle of shop floor. There's the riveter busy driving rivets into the old leg. Eh?

He offered his laugh round the room. The minister continued smiling and Tosh nodded appreciatively. The welder grew strong on this morsel of encouragement.

—Sure, wasn't he doing their work for them? I don't know what they're complaining about.

—Possibly they're jealous of your colleague's craftsmanship, said the doctor drily, still reading *The Times*. The Reverend Harry Legge laughed, for the first time, and the welder eagerly, though belatedly, joined him.

—You remind me of a chap I met once, said the Reverend Legge like a ventriloquist's dummy, —who inadvertently left his limb on a bus, wrapped up in brown paper.

Tosh missed the rest of the anecdote as Armstrong had reappeared.

—Now Mr. Tosh, he said, If you'll come over to the bars.

The parallel bars ran at waist level along one side of the room. At the entrance to them there was a chair and on the wall where they ended there was a mirror from floor to ceiling. Armstrong motioned him into the chair and he set aside the crutches.

—This here's your stump sock, said the limb-fitter, holding a conical, white woollen garment. —You pull it over the stump and it acts as a cushion and a sweat absorber between the stump and the limb socket. Now the leg's held on by this pelvic band that buckles on your abdomen – it should be down over your hip bones and not too tight. This shoulder-strap attaches to it by these studs. A pylon limb doesn't bend when you walk, but to let you sit down, there's this lever half-way down at the back. You pull it with your fingers and it unlocks the knee hinge. When you stand up again and straighten the leg, it snaps shut so you can walk again. Okay?

Tosh nodded. The thing was grotesque.

—If you stand up then, we'll try it on for size.

He stood and the limb-fitter eased him into the socket and did up the belt and strap. Just like your mammy tying your shoe-lace.

—How does that feel, now?

—I don't know. It just feels odd.

—The idea is to catch you on this bone here. He pressed into a point just underneath Tosh's buttock. —You feel that? Now that allows you to *sit* on the leg. Put your weight down... not bad. You're slightly out of it, but you'll settle in after you've walked a bit. Now. Put your hands on these bars, they'll take most of your weight. You can see how you're doing in the mirror. Take a step with your good leg, then bring the other one up alongside it.

Tosh did so.

—That's fine. Keep going like that.

The pylon limb's wooden foot wavered all over the place when he lifted it off the ground. It seemed impossible to control it. He stared raptly down at it, as it moved uncertainly into and out of his vision. It seemed to have only the remotest connection to his will. It kept grazing the ground and he had to hitch up his shoulder to let it swing clear. Then it would swing crazily to one side, stopping him short. He looked up. He was at the mirror. His face looked porous and lined in the fluorescent light, tiny spikes of bristles on his cheeks and chin. Need a shave. He shuffled round and started back. The limb-fitter was watching him. —Don't worry about taking full steps at the moment. Bring the pylon limb up to meet your own leg. The first thing is to get your balance.

He reached the chair again. —Keep going like that for a while, said the limb-fitter. I want you to tell me if you feel too much pressure anywhere, if it starts to hurt you.

After four more journeys down to the mirror and back the foot was beginning to stabilise and Tosh felt hot and exhausted.

—It's pinching me in the front, he said.

—Here?

—Yes, just along there. Feels too tight.

—I'll get them to let that out. Have a rest for a minute.

Tosh fumbled round for the flat lever, pulled it, and the leg suddenly gave. He sat down hard in the chair, his hand squashed under the metal strut.

—You need to be careful that all your weight's on your good leg when you do that, said the limb-fitter, As well as being certain that there's a chair under you.

The Reverend Palmerston Boyle was appearing round the side of the house dribbling his hat before him like a football, there was no escape. He picked the hat up and drop-kicked it, roaring —Up and undah, up and undah! The hat waddled across the small patch of lawn and fell still near Tosh's deck-chair, becoming suddenly very forlorn.

Through his sun-glasses, Tosh watched the jovial head with its natural tonsure and the expression of a schoolboy simpleton, all grins and witlessness, bearing down on him.

—Is your good mother at home? The voice was booming and the vowels pontifically tortured.

—She's inside, said Tosh. Doing her washing.

The Reverend Boyle sat down on the wooden chair beside Tosh and produced cigarettes.

—I was up yesterday moorning... visiting Jimmay McClure, he said, lighting up and picking up his hat from the lawn. —The talk came raund... Uhm... to sheaving. He flicked ash into the upturned hat on his knee. —Now, I... have nevva had a decent sheave... since the old cut-throats went out. These new safety rezas... He beamed benevolently at the assembled garden and laughed pointlessly. —At any rate, Jimmay heppened to mention... ah, that he wet his reza before, ah, sheaving with it.

Tosh's mother appeared at the backdoor of the house.

—I thought I heard your voice, Mr. Boyle, she said in the peculiar simpering tone reserved for professional visitors. —Would you like to come in for a cup of tea? This fellow has another caller.

It was Prudence. She was coming round the side of the house in a dowdy tweed outfit. He had noticed the nose of a car appearing in the street and wondered about it.

—Gave me the closest sheave I've had for years, said the Reverend Boyle.

Tosh looked at him, baffled and seething with repressed vehemence.

—What about... the little matter, asked the Reverend Boyle *sotto voce*, gesturing towards Tosh's whole leg.

—It's all right. I went to the hospital.

Prudence was hovering at a distance. The Reverend Boyle donned his hat and swept towards her.

—Second house! he bellowed, Seats up front! and rushed on into the house.

She came towards him, she looked gaunt in red lipstick, it didn't seem right for a waif. It didn't seem right that such a tiny person could drive the power in a car.

—You're back, he said.

You've had it from me by word of mouth, by demeanour, by letter, everything short of physical assault, but you're not giving up, I have it all to do still.

—I hope you're not cross at me for coming. I just wanted to see how you're keeping.

—Sit down. I'm growing fat.

—You don't look it. But you look much better.

She laughed slightly and prettily.

—I had an awful time finding my way here, she said. So many streets!

—How was vacation work?

The grey look on her face told him about the letter from him that had blighted her summer, stating explicitly, with a cruel clumsiness, what had been implicit in their last encounter.

—It was a nice place, she said, I'm glad to be back.

His mother appeared bearing a tea-tray. His mother disliked Prudence, for a fit of hysteria she had thrown outside the hospital ward, for her monopolising visiting hours, for her designs on a mother's son. The tea-tray was placed on the low garden table in silence and they were left alone again.

—I'm afraid your mother doesn't approve of me.

—Her nerves are bad, she doesn't like anybody.

—I made a bit of a fool of myself in the hospital. It just came over me. I was selling the magazine that afternoon and Harrison walked up and said they'd taken your leg off, I just wasn't prepared for it.

—Don't worry about it.

—When I got to the ward all your family was there and they weren't letting anybody in, and I just went to pieces.

She chewed her lip.

—Your uncle took me home. He was very nice to me.

He poured tea for her.

—You know the strangest thing about a hospital ward? he said. It's just like an airport, or a boat terminal. The most public places in the world and yet the places where people are most trapped in themselves.

She sipped at her tea, and looked down into it.

—The beds are all in rows, he said, But everybody believes that their suffering's unique to themselves, it can't be shared, and what's happening to all the others is just an abstraction called pain or sickness, not the real actual hell that they're in. And the visitors all grieve for their own private person, but all this private grief is going on in a vast company of isolated grieving visitors. Just the way, when you're meeting people off a plane or a train and you're hugging them joyfully, you're surrounded by hordes of other people joyfully hugging, and each person believes that the plane and the airport and the hugs are all specifically for them. If you step back and observe in these places, you get a kind of desperate, hilarious feeling that we're all identical heads on a single body, but none of us can conceive that, because all the heads are blind. We've got everything in common including a conviction of personal uniqueness. There's that constant high pitch of emotion in the air and it all seems fake and histrionic because it isn't shared. Just an endless sequence of little detonations, going on all round you.

It was the longest speech he had made in an age and it surprised him as much as her.

—No wonder porters get cynical, he added lamely.

—Anyway, he said, God knows how many people are losing control of their grief in hospital wards at this moment. So there's no reason in the world why you should feel dismayed that you did.

He was aware that there was no great comfort in being reassured that you're just the same as everybody else, but he felt fairly certain that she wasn't attuned to what he'd been saying, and that the fact of his talking at all to her at such length was reassurance enough in itself.

—I know now that it was selfish, she said, Just adding to everybody else's burden. But it was the shock of it, I couldn't stop myself.

They sipped tea for a few moments.

—I saw Harrison, she said, You're getting a flat together?

—That's the plan.

—You're going to come back to university?

—I suppose I am. It hasn't occurred to me not to.

He knew what was in her mind: she was trying to envision the future.

The day began with the bed jolting as Harrison kicked it to wake him up. Then the smell of toast and the grey light from the back yard. Such a slight transition from sleeping into waking, you could slide back and forward between them twenty times in a minute. The pylon limb propped against the bed-head, with his clothes over it. He'd put an old sneaker over the heavy crescent of wood to disguise it, to stop people's eyes from riveting to it. The woman in the bookstore asked him had he broken his leg on holiday, it was easy to say yes, easy to accede to whatever was called for.

There was the revue to write. Funny songs.

They sat around the fire-place, making remarks. People kept dropping in to be entertained by them, bringing a few Guinness to feed their flip, artificial patter about themselves.

—I'm giving you an oil can for your birthday.

—Make it head oil, the head needs it more than the leg.

—The leg's creaking.

—The head's creaking more.

—It's all this rain, you're rusting in the rain.

—Old Dad Upstairs's crying for his sins.

—He's not crying, he's pissing himself on us.

—He does like a nice smile, don't you, Dad?

—It's our Banana Skin Department.

—It's the hair in the kiss routine.

—It's the way he always gets you when you aren't looking, even when you are looking.

—He hasn't got you recently, you're laughing.

—No, that's true. I'm due.

—Apart from the environmental water-melon.

—Which is always with us.

—Something to get your teeth into.

—It explains all those women who've enervated my youth, starting with the first one who took me, in a graveyard when I was fourteen. You can't win, with a melon like that in your environment.

—Don't sweat it, the tuborg-coloured spectacles'll see you through.

Tosh idled on his guitar for hours. The others involved in the revue came round, feeding each other ideas in slowly accelerating uproar. The funny songs grew out of Tosh's listless, restive mind, crude parodies, gaudy seedless fruit. Sometimes in the early hours, the flat finally empty, they would lie each in his bed in the dark, talking through the open doors of their rooms, listening to jazz from a foreign station on the new radio that Tosh's brother had given him in hospital. Day and night were transitions as slight as waking and sleeping, there was never any knowing the name of the month or the day.

One day he sat in the union with a cup of the coffee that was like muddy drizzle. Harrison came in, looking more stricken than usual.

—Old Dad has achieved another coup.

He hunched down on a bench, lighting a cigarette and inhaling it sharply.

—The flat's been bust into. They came up the back yard and knocked a hole in the window.

—What'd they take?

—They took your radio.

No. No.

—That was apparently all they were after, because it was new obviously. They could see it through the window sitting on the fireplace. It must have been those two creeps who came to the backdoor asking for old clothes the other day, they were obviously checking the place out. They just waited till we both went out, then nipped up through the yard, cracked the window, grabbed it and ran.

A heavier blow than it should be; crushing in fact. His brother's unarticulated anguish and concern, all invested in the gift of the radio, had been violated and mocked. He felt the inconsolable weight of his brother's love, and an unreasonable, relentless guilt for the loss of the radio. It should never have been left on the fire-place, in view of the window.

It wasn't the radio. It was the pathos of what the radio represented to him.

—I suppose we'd better report it.

—I phoned the police already, they're sending up a detective. I'd better get back in case he's there already.

—I'll come with you.

He was numbed by his powerlessness, rendered stupid and vague by it.

Before the revue opened, they went drinking. When he found himself on the stage, he couldn't remember where they had gone or for how long. The audience was jammed in and very noisy. After they started the opening song, the noise increased, a constant barrage of catcalls and jokes from drunks, other parts of the audience arguing with them, and a press of people trying to squeeze in at the door. Tosh went on performing with the others, mechanically, aware that only the first few rows could hear him over the bedlam. He began to feel that all the sound in the large basement was coming from the audience, that for all his straining, nothing but silence flowed from his own mouth and hands. It was as if he was looking out at them from a fish tank, his mouth slowly opening and closing in a constant O, and all their rage and turmoil filtering in through the troubled water.

Occasionally the noise would diminish, and they would surface briefly into a moment of calm, the players performing and the audience responding, like a sleeper momentarily realising that he's merely having a nightmare. Then one of the drunks would call out, some of the audience would laugh, other wags would try to emulate the first, some of the audience would tell them to shut up, and the derangement of swirling pandemonium would be in action again.

Harrison prowled in the wings, the spring of his resentment coiling. Finally he burst onto the stage in the middle of a skit and spat out —All right, that's it! at the audience. His voice wasn't particularly loud, but the venomous aura that he projected induced an abrupt silence.

—We worked our arses off to give you this show. The least you could do is give it a hearing. You're not worth it. You don't deserve it. As far as I'm concerned, the show's over.

He came off, like a piece of wire pulled out of a fire, white and dangerous. The audience sat on, transfixed and still. —I'm prepared to try it again, said one of the cast on the stage, —If everybody else is. There were subdued voices assenting from the auditorium. The skit began again in a frozen calm, and the revue proceeded to its close, with the audience laughing and applauding on cue. There was the brittle gaiety of a party after a guest has made a fool of himself and been angrily rebuked by the host. It was in its way even more unreal than the preceding hubbub, the audience was acting more deliberately than the players, Tosh felt himself addressing a chastised classroom. It seemed that the evening would never reach its end. He could sense already the failure of a previously hidden nerve: he would never again be able to get up before an audience and perform with an unconscious faith in the easy security of his own stage presence. The world no longer offered security, of any sort whatsoever.

His father called each Saturday after noon to take him home for the week-end. It was a journey into metallic luminosity, the light from the television filling the living-room, its electric spell hardening round them as the long evening twilight wore on. On the screen the little figures in dark suits hurried about in their own harshly monochromatic world, looking steadily at each other for much of the time, shooting each other. Their flat curt voices spoke tonelessly through the dead air of the room like voices heard at the edge of anaesthesia. The theme music, the heavy bass pulse under a snarl of brass, music of police sirens and whining gears and bodies pummelling one another, held them in the thrall of its hypnotic familiarity.

At home at the week-ends Tosh found it impossible to remember what he had been doing during the week. After returning to the flat on Sunday nights, he had no clear recollection of the week-end.

Higgins came back from one of his crazy travel adventures and they went drinking.

—What'd you do to your leg? he asked.

—I had it sawn off.

—Oh aye, that's right. He scratched the pimple on his nose reflectively. —I suppose it must have been a bit sore.

—I'm still not sure whether I died or not.

—Gosh.

Tosh laughed deeply at Higgins, half in incredulity at the world he carried round with him, like a magnetic field magically shielding him from all calamity. It was compounded of innocence and good timing, a ponderous recklessness, an avuncular hedonism: uncomplicated and incomprehensible. Higgins led a charmed life, cruising blithely unscathed through the most deadly situations, passing exams that he hadn't taken, winning the physical favours of virtually every woman to whom he made his derisory, ludicrous advances.

—I was standing in this chemist's in Turkey, he said, Trying to buy something to cure the runs, when this big lump of blubber runs in. Huge creature, so he was. He was jabbering away at the top of his voice. Couldn't understand a word.

—Was he Turkish?

—No, he was Australian. Anyway, he grabs this disinfectant off the shelf, whips down the bags, and pours the whole bottle of stuff over his testimonials. Right there in the shop. The chemist goes berserk and pushes him out into the street with the trousers down round his ankles. It was lucky I was there or he would have been done for.

—Why, what'd you do?

—I told him to pull up his trousers. Then I took him to a bogs to wash himself off. He'd been lured into a whore-house by some tragic bit of scrag and the place was so pigging he was convinced he was riddled so he just charged out screaming into the chemist's. He was a bit on the dense side, if you ask me.

—I stowed away on a boat from Penang to Madras, he said. We got fed up hiding after the first night. So we just started strolling around, acting very nonch. This steward suddenly heads towards us and just as we're about to make a run for it, he says the captain sends word that we're invited to lunch and dinner with him. The only whites on board, you see. So we spent the rest of the voyage playing rummy in the first-class lounge. That sort of discrimination's disgusting.

—How'd you get off at the other end?

—We claimed that we'd already disembarked and then gone back to get our rucksacks. They didn't believe us but we got swept away in the crowd and made a dash for it.

The evening grew delirious. They got caught up in twitting a group of rugby fans.

—Give me a good ballet any day, said Higgins.

—Just because *you're* a fairy, Higgins, said a wiry rugby fan in horn-rimmed spectacles.

—Admit it, said Tosh, You're all deeply anxious about your virility and you'd rather have the rough male kiss of a blanket than face a woman.

—That's Rupert Brooke, said Higgins, He was a rugby player too.

—He was a weedy poof like you, said the rugby fan.

—Give us a kiss, said Higgins.

—I'll give you a pasting, it's bloody well what you're asking for.

—What it all proves, said Tosh, Is that your development was arrested at the anal stage. Thrashing about in the mud is just a sublimation of eating your shit.

—You're going to get your face pushed in, said the rugby fan, pulling Tosh towards him by the tee-shirt.

—Go ahead, hit me, said Tosh unctuously, I understand your needs. But I have to warn you. This leg is the property of the Ministry of Health. Damage it, and you'll be answerable to them for the consequences.

—Is this your idea of fair play? asked Higgins rhetorically of the other rugby fans, —Standing by while one of your number threatens a man with an artificial leg?

—I didn't know about his damned leg, said the aggressor, dropping his hand.

—Come on, hit me, said Tosh heatedly. Maybe you think I'm some kind of a cripple?

—How was I to know? muttered the rugby fan, turning away to his drink.

—What happened to your leg? asked one of the discomfited fans, in a placatory voice.

Tosh drank moodily.

—It's not a pretty story, he said, lighting a cigarette.

At closing time the fans invited them to a party. Higgins had his mother's car, and they drove behind the others bumping them gently in the rear every thirty yards, hooting with laughter like two kids in a fair-ground. The white faces in front scowled and mouthed at them through the rear window, approaching and receding like a wave.

The wide, wide footpath seemed to stretch away from him for miles, glistening in its oily coating of rain. The dead leaves were shedding down into it, all he had to do was to put his pylon foot or the tip of his walking stick on a wet leaf, and he'd be down with a crack, hip torn from its socket, maybe. The yellowy brown leaves stuck as they fell. He would have to walk the whole length, picking his way between the leaves with tensed, gingerly steps. It would take an age of caution.

The street was transformed by snow in the morning and it crunched under him easily enough, it was dry and fluffy. He was indoors all day while it was slowly scarred black by the traffic, and turned into slushy grey glar that got packed down onto the footpaths under passing feet. He had a late tutorial with a tall, benevolent man called Dr. Dodds, whose skin was sallow and hairless, and whose voice was unexpectedly piping. By the time this was over, the lights were on for dusk, and it was freezing outside and the twilight full of swirling flakes.

—Can you manage in the snow, asked Dr. Dodds, lighting his pipe and gesturing with the dead match towards Tosh's leg.

—I'll take it slowly, said Tosh, My flat's fairly close.

—I do wish I could offer you transportation, but alas I have none.

—That's all right.

—Never mind, I'll walk with you.

—That's very kind, but I'll be okay, really.

—No, I will, those footpaths can be very treacherous.

They emerged into the half-light where the still-hard snow which had set on the ground was buffed by the eddying gusts of wild flakes. Tosh moved cautiously down the path, feeling himself on a carpet that might be jerked away at any moment. At the end his feet slithered a little and his whole body tightened. He didn't want to risk another step. He breathed deeply and shuffled forward a little till he could hold on to the railing. Dr. Dodds, buttoning his tweed overcoat, came down the path saying

—The Augustans made far more sophisticated distinctions than we do. Look at all their varieties of literary mockery.

They began walking, Tosh keeping his guarded steps as slow and short as he could.

—They did a good line in invective, he murmured.

—Oh quite, the most scurrilous ever written, said Dr. Dodds enthusiastically, That was the raw substance of their lowest forms. The lampoon. The crudely polemical or personal broadside ballad. But then above that...

Tosh's pylon leg skidded out at an angle, he fell askew onto his other knee and his hands.

—Whoops, careful, said Dr. Dodds.

Like the slow agony of a heavy punch below the belt, the pain of the twisted stump robbed him of breath. He straightened up gasping.

—Are you hurt?

—I'll be all right... in just a minute. He felt sick and weak from the pain which kept unfolding like a stain.

—Hold on to my shoulder, said the tutor, You're really not fit to be out in these conditions.

—I've just... strained myself a bit. He pushed his weight down on the pylon leg. The pain was ebbing slightly. His hands were numb from the snow, but his body felt clammy.

—I think I'm able to press on, he said presently.

—Here, lean on my arm.

He wrapped his hand round the tutor's tweedy, thin forearm and they lurched off slowly.

—They had high and low forms of parody too, said Dr. Dodds. Burlesque and mock-heroic right up to dignified pastiche, the lofty imitations of classical poets.

—Their society was so rigid, though, said Tosh, Surely that was why they could achieve those refinements. Wasn't that the price of it?

—It was far less rigid than you think, there was considerable social mobility...

—But the elite culture of the coffee-houses, most of the people must have been oblivious of it...

His leg again sheared off to one side, he threw his weight on the supporting arm, they both tottered a little.

—Sorry.

—Steady up. Are you all right?

—Fine.

—We must have all the appearance of two drunks.

They reached the head of the street where the flat was. The packed snow on the footpath here was bumpy and uneven. It had been out of reach of the afternoon sun. With every step now, Tosh slid a little. Dr. Dodds was holding his arm with both hands, taking most of his weight, half-carrying him. Tosh kept his eyes on the foot of crusted rock-hard ice in front of him, willing himself to be home.

—Yes, there was certainly a highly developed social structure, said Dr. Dodds. Not the kind of thing we approve of today. And yes, it was a society that perpetrated terrible evils and cruelties. But I know of no society that didn't or doesn't. Whereas I know of few which bequeathed to posterity such a radiant sense of order, such a civilised set of distinctions.

—It's the order we feel most wistful about today, said Tosh, All those lost souls in their neo-Georgian property developments listening to Vivaldi on the hi-fi.

Dr. Dodds laughed, a falsetto triplet.

—Very good, Mr. Tosh, though perhaps a trifle glib.

—I don't mean it to be, said Tosh, I'm one of them, except that I don't have the house or the record player.

Dr. Dodds laughed again, with more reserve. They came to a halt.

—Is this your flat?

—Will you come in and have some tea?

—Thank you, but I'm expected home. I've enjoyed our chat.

They shook hands.

—You saved my bacon, said Tosh, I could never have made it alone.

—We must do it again. It's very good for an academic to do something actually useful once in a while. If you need an arm, just shout.

—I will.

—For heaven's sake don't try to manage on your own, not in weather like this, he said, starting back up the windy, shrouded street.

—I couldn't do it on my own. Thank you again.

He sat immobile in Aggie Dobbs' exam and wondered vaguely why he had turned up for it at all. The questions were foreign and undecipherable to him, all of them, they were bound to be, he'd done no preparation for them. It was an automatic reflex that brought you in. You knew there wasn't a single word you could write on the paper, yet you walked in with your pen in your pocket and carefully studied the questions. He was going through the accepted motions of acquiring an education, with every faculty operating except for his mind. His mind had moved away, had left no forwarding address, had taken his will along with it. Husk in the wind. Aggie Dobbs was bent over her desk. Her eyes seemed to have withered away behind her blue wing-tip spectacles. She was an academic spinster, weaned on gall.

The others toyed abstractedly with the questions, the usual few writing busily. If you walk out they'll look up intrigued and whisper in concern, he wanted to remain unobtrusive. But you can't sit like this for two hours. You could write gibberish but what about handing it in? Anything. Who cares. Mullen had dropped something at his feet. He picked it up. A note. *I'll give you a few bits and pieces to cover yourself.* He looked at Aggie, she was still bent over the desk. If she could detect that his answers were taken from Mullen she'd be venomous. He could disguise them, though, camouflage them. Who cares. Mullen was witty and devious, with little interest in his studies, he'd only have a few rudiments to offer anyway. *O.K. I'll change it around so she won't catch you on,* Tosh scribbled and pushed the note back. With astonishing speed, Aggie Dobbs was down and had the exchange of notes in her hand. Oh Christ. Curse it. She had taken it back to the desk, was reading it. She swept out of the room with it.

Mullen and Tosh exchanged pained glances. To be caught out like schoolboys at this stage. It was going to be derisively embarrassing. It was your fault for turning up at all, you helpless fool.

The Professor's head appeared round the door, the eyes as usual quizzically wide over the tops of the spectacles.

—Er, Mr. Mullen and Mr... er, Tosh, will you come up to my study?

Mullen groaned, and smiled sheepishly at the pale, alerted faces of the others. They started up the stairs.

—I'll talk, said Tosh, You say nothing.

The Professor was seated at his desk, gazing myopically into the middle distance. There was no sign of Aggie Dobbs. They were gestured towards seats.

—This is a most unfortunate incident, said the Professor. He seemed unable to think of anything to add to this.

—The blame's entirely mine, sir, said Tosh, hearing the words mocking him with their ring of decent-chappishness. —I'd done no work at all for the exam. I should never have shown up for it. Mullen... had nothing to do with it.

—Yes, said the Professor. Well, I'm not going to take this any further. I'm assuming that you'll apologise to Miss Dobbs. She's... considerably upset by it.

—Yes, sir.

—Good, good. Well. Carry on.

When they had reached the door, the Professor leaned across his desk.

—Ah... Mr. Tosh. If you get into difficulties, as a result of your... unhappy accident... this isn't the way to resolve them.

—No, sir.

The Professor leaned back in his seat and resumed his vague unfocused gaze. They closed the door quietly behind them.

—Jesus. That wasn't too bad, said Mullen.

—Aggie's probably up in her study, said Tosh. We might as well go right up and eat shit for her.

—Yeah, get it over with.

They climbed the remaining two flights of stairs to the small landing at the top of the building, took a deep breath, and knocked on the door of the little office. There was no reply.

—She must be back in the exam, said Mullen.

—What'll we do?

—We might as well wait.

They lit up cigarettes and leaned on the banister, talking sporadically. There wasn't much to say. The situation was ludicrous but extremely discomfiting. At last they heard the exam breaking up two floors below them, and steps coming up the stairs. Aggie Dobbs' grey head appeared beneath them, bobbing upwards. They straightened themselves and stood stiffly as she came level.

—Miss Dobbs, Mullen and I would like to say...

She moved on past icily, opened her door and slammed it behind her without a word. Tosh shrugged. They descended the stairs in silence.

—What does the oul bag want us to do? said Mullen at the door, We've made the gesture, anyway.

—I'll approach her again, she'll come round, said Tosh. Listen, thanks for trying and I'm very sorry indeed to have landed you in this.

—I'd do it again, for Jesus' sake, said Mullen through his teeth, grinning, —Three years from now, Aggie Dobbs'll mean nothing to either one of us, and all that compost heap that she calls required source material – in the name of gentle Jesus, what use will that be to anybody, living or dead?

Tosh laughed his agreement. But after Mullen was gone, he felt the incident cloaking him like a heavy miasma.

The next afternoon he ascended again to Aggie Dobbs' garret study. Again she was out and again he waited. When she came bobbing up the stairs this time, she forestalled him by announcing —I've nothing to say to *you*, with a note of contempt, and closed the door in his face. There seemed little point in persevering.

But a few days later he encountered her coming towards him on the pavement.

—Miss Dobbs, he said.

She walked slightly past him and then stopped.

—Well, what do you have to say for yourself? she asked acidly.

—I wanted to say... it's difficult to frame an explanation which doesn't sound like a silly excuse.

—Quite.

He took a breath and looked her in the face.

—I've been living in... an odd kind of vacuum. Nothing has meant very much to me this past while. The morning before the exam my flat was broken into and a radio stolen, which doesn't sound like much but it was a major blow... I won't try to explain why, I'm not very sure why. Anyway, none of this is meant to exonerate me. It's just the sort of climate in which I was functioning or failing to function. I didn't do any work for the exam. Mullen was distressed at me being so clearly lost. We both offer apologies, but I'm the one who's the culprit and I... take the blame... and I'm especially sorry for having... hurt your feelings.

Her thin tight mouth and dead eyes showed no signs of softening.

—I'm a cunning old fox, she said, You won't get very much past me.

Tosh could think of no suitable reply, and looked down at his feet.

—I'm too old to play tricks on, she said, What does Mullen have to say for himself?

—He wanted to tender his apologies also.

She looked at him steadily, the impression of a cold glint somewhere in her features.

—You were idiots to try such a thing on me. However, I'll accept your apologies.

She was gone. He limped on down the street thinking, Another glorious chapter of your education brought to a close.

The chestnut tree was across the street from the library window, beside a street lamp. The bark of the sturdy trunk was glistening and muscular, like the velvety sweating flank of a dark-brown horse. The rain was falling very gently, in the darkness it was imperceptible. But the tree's great leafy bole was glistening with it, the droplets catching the light of the street lamp forming concentric patterns like those of iron filings in the field of a magnet. Such peace exists in the natural course of things. Such magnificent repose. I can perceive this. It exists in my awareness of it. Such order. It must be present somewhere in yourself, for you to recognise it so.

He was rapt in the utter stillness of the tree, no leaf stirring, no jewel of rain seeming to fall from the tip of a leaf. And yet the tree had a sense of profound energy to it. The tree conducts its own life, whether you attend to it or not. The tree and the rain, and the lamp which made them radiant. You spy on them through your window. Voice them in your head, from the midst of soiled books and relentless light.

—Try it outside the bars and keep walking for fifteen minutes or so. I want to see if any discomfort develops.

The limb-fitter left the room. Tosh stepped out from between the parallel bars and steadied himself. It was slightly unnerving to be faced by the empty room, to launch yourself into a space unbounded by the security of wooden rails. He walked along beside the rails at first, touching the outer one lightly with each step. The imitation leg obediently swung at its knee below him and took his weight when he shifted on to it. He turned at the wall and went back across the room, further away from the rails this time. It was all right. His walking became more relaxed and confident and he strode at an angle across the room and back again at a different angle.

—Man alive, that's great. It was the first words spoken by the only other occupant of the Fitting Room. —That's powerful altogether, is that your first leg?

—The first articulated one, said Tosh.

—The what?

—I've been going round on a pylon leg but this is the first real one.

The man was in his sixties and had sparse ginger hair and a simple, intent pink face. He didn't seem to know what a pylon leg was.

—What happened you? he asked.

—Cancer.

—Son dear. That's bad luck. You're walking great though, you would hardly know you'd ever lost it.

He watched with the unnatural concentration of someone who has a constant fear that they're being left behind. His pink right leg ended in a bony purple point at the ankle.

—Mine was a crash, he said. I was coming home from work on my bike and this joker in a van comes flying round a corner far too wide and before I knew anything about it I was on my face on the deck and he was over my foot.

The words were worn smooth and comfortable with use, Tosh could hear them being recited again and again in a hospital ward. The limb-fitter reappeared bearing a tin foot and ankle with a lot of leather harness on it.

—Now, Mr. Lyttle, are you going to walk for us this week?

—Right you are, doctor.

The man blinked rapidly and sat up straight on the edge of his chair.

—Come over to the bars and we'll get you strapped in, said the limb-fitter, lifting the man and tucking his wooden crutches under his arms.

Tosh sat down, partly to give the man a clear path to the rails, and partly because the leg had begun to dig painfully into his groin. The man edged slowly on his crutches to the head of the parallel rails and stood there while the limb-fitter strapped on his leg.

—Now, said the limb-fitter straightening up. Just edge yourself forward. You're totally safe, there's no way you can fall.

As Tosh watched, the man stood irresolute, staring in fear at his full-length reflection at the other end of the rails. There were freckles on his face and thin pink thighs. He wore no underpants and his genitals hung beneath the short shirt forlorn and pathetic, like the wattles of dead turkeys in a butcher's window. To be face to face with such an image of yourself. Pilloried. The first sight of it.

—A wee step with your good foot'll get you started, said the limb-fitter. Go ahead, you're all right.

—That boyo there can walk anyway, the man said shakily. Eh? He can fairly skite around.

At last he shifted forward, lurching on his arms which were bearing most of his weight. He trembled slightly as he inched and jerked down towards the pitiless depths of the mirror.

Armstrong came in.

—What's this, slacking off? he said grinning at Tosh.

—It was cutting into me on the inside.

—Stand up till I have a look.

Tosh stood up and the limb-fitter probed and prodded round the inner rim of the leg's socket.

—Put your weight on it. Aye, you're sliding down into the socket. Your stump must have shrunk more.

He stepped back. —Take it off and I'll get another lining put in it.

An hour later Tosh emerged into the world, moving with a gingerly limp on a stick, with a whole body again to all appearances.

He paced from the bed to the kitchen door, to the sink beside it, to the little pantry, back to the bed, to the dead fire-place. Anything was funny if you could view it from the proper position. If you couldn't, it wasn't. He paced back into the kitchen and looked through the thick grime on the window. If it wasn't, there was no savour. At best, tedium. Maybe you should go away, start again on new premises. But what would you go towards? And you'd carry the same cargo wherever you went, no way to jettison it. He moved to the bed again and stared into the grate. Every night a dream of fast running, steady running, then sudden fall: jolted awake, with the heart pounding. You have to be prudent. You have to move with extreme care.

The door-bell rang, he went. It was Florence, a sometimes partner of Harrison's. Prudence's friend. Frizz of dark hair, big freckles, eyes slightly protruding, full lips.

—He isn't here, said Tosh. He's away someplace.

—I just wondered how you both were keeping.

—C'mon in.

She sat in a chair by the empty fire-place.

—I haven't seen you since the revue, she said. I thought it was really very good, even though I was raging at those creeps in the audience.

—I'd forgotten all about it.

—You should do it again.

Tosh winced and shook his head.

—No, really, you should. Those songs, as such, were really very funny. I'd like to hear the bits I missed.

He gave her a cigarette.

—What have you been doing since? she asked.

—Simmering very slowly in my own juice, he said.

—You sound a bit depressed.

—I can't stand my own mind, he said with intensity. It's a stew of self-pity and self-abuse, and feeble inaction, it churns on and on and on and produces nothing. I feel totally alone. I'm lonely, he said.

She looked at him, her eyes agitated, a flush coming into her thickly freckled cheeks.

—You? she said. Not you, love. You know dozens of people.

—I don't know anybody. I don't know you. Who are you?

She returned his stare for a few moments, blinking rapidly, then looked away.

—I just can't believe — as such — you, of all people.

—I didn't mean to frighten you, said Tosh.

—There are so many friends you could call on.

—It's not the body that's lonely, even though it is insatiable. I've been making that mistake all along myself.

—Have you been feeling like this since — the leg?

—It started before that. Two cankers that just happened to grow together. Or maybe that's the way it always works, I don't know.

They sat in strained silence.

—Have you had your tea yet? said Tosh.

—No, not as such.

—Neither have I, so why don't I make some for both of us. If you can stand my dismal company for another half-hour.

—Let me make it. I'd like to, really I would. What's in the larder?

—Eggs, I think.

She was already in the kitchen, checking.

—Four eggs, one carrot and a tin of creamed rice, she called in. I think reinforcements are called for. I'll go and get some more eggs and mushrooms and whatnot and do you an omelette. Okay?

—Take some money.

—Treat's on me, back in a jiffy.

You could fantasise a perfect room, of course, an ideal woman, a contented state of being, you do it all the time. Projecting all the fleeting intimations into an impossible actuality. Foolish chimeras. But real, as real as the constant tingling and twinging in the shin and sole and instep of your non-existent leg. It's what keeps you nourished. A thin diet of day-dreams. While life slowly kills you. Why is it all set up like that? Give it a rest, belly-ache.

Florence came back, bearing too much food, a bottle of wine and a bright smile. Determined to cure the malcontent. She lit the candle stubs in the empty wine bottles and cracked saucers still on the mantelpiece from the last party.

She cooked as he laid the table. —Harrison's so childish, she said, I think he stuck at the age of fourteen and he's never going to grow any older. He puts on such a silly act, he really does, I just get fed up.

As she ate, she said, —The funny thing about me is, that I never really sit and think over my life, as such, at all. I mean, I think about each thing that happens, but I couldn't truthfully say overall whether I was happy or not. I suppose I am, really. I just don't think about it.

Over the last of the wine she said, —Every so often I get a sinking feeling about the future. It's all right for somebody creative like you, I mean, you'll always be able to make a place for yourself, as such, whatever you do. I'm just no good at anything, God alone knows how I'll get through life. A candle spluttered, drowning in its final pool of wax, and expired.

He studied the plump, mobile curve of her cheek as she washed the dishes and talked, and as he dried them, standing a little behind her. He followed her back into the room and before she sat down, he said:

—Florence, would you mind if I kissed you?

—No, not at all, she said, with a look of alarm.

They kissed awkwardly twice, standing up, and then sprawled across the bed and she nestled into him. Another dying candle butt fell down into its bottle, crackled and went out.

—Tosh, she whispered at length, What exactly is it you want from life? I know the leg must have been a shattering blow. We were devastated by it, all of us. But you've recovered so well, and you've got so much else on your side. I mean, your life as such is almost as it was, just as if nothing had happened. What is it you want?

Short intermission.

—I'm looking for signs of life.

—How do you mean?

—I've been away a fearful distance, Florence. I want to come back to life. I can't do it alone. I need some soul to meet me.

—Soul?

—Don't get alarmed. I'm a faithful subject of the secular realm. It's all saints and martyrs otherwise, I'm not attracted to either option. But I know my body's a behaviourist puppet... as such. He smiled. —The mind makes these bones talk. And the words are all we have. And beyond the words and the mind is where you feel you live. An illusory place, probably, a void, a necessary fiction. I'm very attached to that word, soul.

He let his voice die in the hushed dimness of the room. Why go on? Why go back?

—So where do you start, Florence? Where does a soul find its mirror? I'm waiting for the kiss of life. It's only through each other that we even begin to exist at all.

Another candle flickered fitfully, hissed, and petered out, and they were in darkness. He turned towards her.

—Tosh, she whispered. Prudence would like to see you again.

III

From corner to corner across the empty avenues, a scarecrow pendulum on the loose, suspended between the metal crutches, clank of his weary bones. The wind like sudden antlers of ice. His grey coat flaps round the empty space below. Broad streets unfolding endlessly. No moorings. Dwarf hobbling through a wilderness of towering headstones.

The figments of the lost year grind themselves away in his head, and all the city's trees and souls, all the tired grass and exhausted engines, the gaudy rags in the window displays, all the trophies and hunters, and the alley cats and the powdered dogs, all the discarded tickets and torn wrappings dragged around the kerbs by the vulpine wind, they all petrify round him till the whole city is stone, the stone sea bed of a cemetery, and him the only survivor, adrift in a stone forest. Now the sky begins to turn.

> Drop down. Drop. Fall into stone.
> I won't fall. I won't go down till I'm dropped down.
> And he said, I will not let go except thou bless me.

The sky goes granite. He poles his way along by the long railings. Where the railings end there's an old man seated on the stone footpath. Cap beside him, upside down, with coins gleaming on the dark greasy lining. One leg outstretched with his wooden crutches laid beside it. Stump in the cut-off trouser leg.

He watches Tosh slowly swaying along the whole length of the railings towards him, long body dragged by the inexorable rhythm of the crutches. Watches Tosh draw level with him. Winks in recognition.

Tosh pulls off the crutches from his arms and slides down beside the man. Together they look around them. He gives the man a cigarette, takes one for himself.

—What's your story, son? the man asks him then.

So I tell him my story. And at last free. Peace, for a brief spell, at least. Peace.

Parker's Original Plan for the Novel

Some time after he conceived the idea of writing the story of his amputation as a screenplay in February 1970, Parker decided to write it as a novel in 1971 or early 1972. He probably made these notes towards *Caution In the Traffic, Prudence In the Rain* (the book's original title) on 12 January 1972, when he recorded in his journal that he had 'Sketched out rough scheme for Caution.' This 'scheme' consisted of two numbered lists of scenes, along with a couple of potential scenes noted in parentheses at the bottom of the first list. The lists appeared alongside each other in Parker's handwritten plan. I have endeavoured to preserve Parker's spelling and punctuation and have added my own notations in italics.

Prudence In the Rain
1. Tosh enters the Gymnasium
2. McIlwaine in the Union
3. Redpath
4. In the rain, on the quad.
5. With Harrison, the drama festival.
6. Going in, leg shaved.
7. Old lady, in T.'s mind
8. Old lady, objective

Items 6-8 are bracketed together on the right side, with a 3. written farther to the right.

9. Easter holiday.
10. At the doctor's. *This item has a 1. written off to the right of it.*
11. Rag Day
12. Collapse of leg. *This item has a 2. written off to the right of it.*
13. Pubic hair shaved, 1st.operation *This item has a 4.written off to the right of it.*
14. Sailing
15. Prudence's last 2 visits
16. Eve. before the amputation
17. What Is the Ocean Doing?
18. Phantasmagoria

(Invit. from Prof) *This entry is crossed out.*
(boy at bus stop)
(Party)

Caution In the Traffic
Prologue – date w/ nurse.
1. Ingrid.
2. Pain recurs in other leg –
Second visit to hospital *These were originally separate numbered scenes, but Parker apparently decided almost immediately to combine them.*
3. First visit To Limb Fitting Centre.
4. Naturopath
5. Schoolgirl in magazine
5A. Cora. *This entry was probably added after the original list was made, and the existence of another 'Cora' entry in brackets between scenes 8 and 9 may indicate that Parker had trouble deciding where to put that particular scene.*
6. Evening with Harold Gams.
7. Going home.
8. Formal.
[Cora]
9. Second visit to Limb Fitting Centre: Pylon
10. Prudence in the garden

11. Flat week: revue.
12. Home weekend.
13. Higgins, car – fictitious story about leg.
14. Play production. *This entry is crossed out.*
15. Snow.
16. Exam.

The Tree *This entry seems to have been added late, since it is unnumbered and inserted between two existing entries.*

17. Dishwashing
18. Return to Prudence *This entry is crossed out.*
19. Receiving new leg. *This entry is followed by an arrow indicating that it should go between 'The Tree' and 'Dishwashing'.*
20. Culmination

APPENDIX 2

Revised Order of Scenes

Parker's journal indicates that he began rearranging the scenes of his novel within days of completing the initial draft on 25 September 1973. On 29 September 1973, when most of these notes were likely made, he wrote that he had 'Worked out new sequence of sections for Caution.'

This schema also contains notations Parker made in felt tip at a later date – probably in either 1982 or 1988, since in both those years he returned to the novel with the intention of finishing it. I have indicated these in bold type.

My own notations appear here in italics. Otherwise, I have tried to copy Parker's spelling and punctuation.

In addition to the two numbered lists indicating the order of scenes, this page contains other notes Parker wrote to himself, which I will reproduce below before proceeding to the lists:

Interior passages in 2nd. person.
p.31. Link radio to 'tariff' passage.
<u>Diguises</u> *Presumably Parker meant to write 'Disguises' here.*

Nurse
Ingrid
Schoolgirl
Cora

Sinead

Prudence

Florence *This list of women's names is contained within a bracket.*

What is Ocean Doing in Pt. 2?

Parker's revised lists of scenes, this time marked 'THERE' and 'BACK':

THERE

1. Enter Gymnasium
   True Thomas w/ Larmour.
2. McIlwaine in Union.
   Sleeping Beauty w/ kids
3. Redpath.
4. On the quad.
5. Drama Festival
6. At the doctor's.
7. Easter holiday
8. Collapse of leg.
9. Rag Day. ?
   Boy at bus stop.
10. Going in.
11. Sailing.
    Brendan w/ Larmour
12. Pubic hair shaved. *Parker had crossed out* 'Old Lady' *here.*
    Jacob w/ Rev. Boyle *An arrow after this entry indicates that it should be moved to a spot between items 13 and 14 on this list.*
13. Old Lady.
14. Party.
15. Gillespie.
16. Prudence's last 2 visits.
17. Evening before amputation
18. **Larmour & the sacred texts** *Parker envisaged this scene replacing* 'What Is the Ocean Doing?' *in this spot. The original entry is crossed out, with the new one written above it.*
19. Phantasmagoria.

141

<u>BACK</u>

1. Prologue
2. Going home.
3. Ingrid.
4. Schoolgirl
5. Harold Gambs [*sic*]
6. Cora.
7. Pain recurs.
8. Limb Centre I
9. Prudence in Garden
10. Naturopath.
11. Higgins, car. *This entry is crossed out.*
12. Limb Centre 2. *This entry is crossed out.*
11. Limb Centre 2.
12. Flat week, revue.
13. Home week-end.
14. Formal
15. Exam
15A. Higgins car
16. Snow
17. The Tree *This entry is followed by an arrow indicating that it should be moved to a spot just before the 'Snow' scene.*
18. Dishwashing
19. Receiving new leg.
20. Culmination

At the bottom of the page, Parker listed (in felt tip) several scenes that did not yet exist, putting the whole list in brackets:
Brendan w/ Larmour
Jacob w/ minister
Fat student on picket line. (daemon lover)
Country student's outburst, Mullan.
Jest Book? *This entry probably refers to an earlier unpublished novel by Parker.*

Parker's Final Plan for Hopdance

In 1982, Parker returned to his novel (which he had decided to re-entitle *Hopdance* in 1974, the year before he set it aside indefinitely). At this stage, though, he was doing more thinking about the book than committing words to paper. He applied himself seriously to the task of finishing the novel in the summer and early autumn of 1988, when he made this final plan for it. Items with asterisks beside them on the list of episodes to be included in Part One indicate scenes he had yet to write. He eventually completed scene 3, but the others remained unwritten at the time of his abrupt death from stomach cancer on 2 November 1988. My own notations appear in italics.

<u>Part One</u>
  I. First mirror.
  II. 1. He was a student of literature at that time
     2. On the quad *Parker had crossed out* 'Anybody know "Fair Rosa"?' *here.*
     3. * Fat student on the picket line *Parker had crossed out* 'Redpath' *here.*
     4. Anybody know 'Fair Rosa'? *Parker had crossed out* 'On the quad' *here.*
     5. Redpath

6. Drama Festival
7. * Country student, Mullan.
8. Rag Day. *Parker had crossed out* 'Drama Festival' *here.*
9. At the doctor's
10. Easter Holiday
11. At ten o'clock one morning, Tosh got up from bed
12. We'd like you to come in for a few days, said the surgeon
13. Drizzle outside, the coffee a kind of foamy drizzle
14. In the evening his father drove him
15. They shinned down the mooring rope
16. * Larmour & Brendan *Parker had crossed out* 'Tosh woke up like a blind being raised' *here.*
17. Tosh woke up like a blind being raised
18. * Minister & Jacob
19. Little lady, in her hat
20. He sat, heavy and slow w/ drink
21. The surgeon had iron-grey hair
22. The care of posterity is greatest
23. Much later, Gillespie
24. They came to visit Tosh
25. Tosh hadn't helped his case
*26. Larmour and the sacred texts
27. Phantasmagoria.
III. For three days he had lain objectified

Part Two

I. He puts on the short grey coat
II: 1. The clothes were a tactile rough-house at first
2. Ingrid.
3. I've got it in the other leg
4. Entering was like a beggar's [sic] burlesque of royalty
5. Something fell through with regard to the flat
6. Magazine of a girl's [sic] private school
7. Harold Gambs [sic] at the door one evening

Source Texts for 'Tosh's essay'

Parker's final plan for *Hopdance*, made in 1988, includes an entry for a section labelled 'The care of posterity is greatest' which does not appear on any of his previous lists of scenes. Stuck into the *Hopdance* manuscript at this point in the novel (right after a scene describing Tosh's thoughts and actions on the evening and morning before his amputation) are three separate manuscripts that Parker likely intended to adapt as a representation of the 'fair-sized essay on the state of poetry in contemporary society' that Tosh writes on the morning of the surgery. The first, in Parker's mature handwriting and using the kind of paper and pen he favoured at the end of his life, is a fragment probably written around the same time as the other late additions to the novel in 1988. The second, dated 17 May 1966, was evidently written on the fifth anniversary of Parker's amputation, although I do not know whether or not it represented an attempt to recreate an essay he himself might have written immediately before the loss of his leg. He had discovered it among his papers in 1979, at which time he had no memory of writing it, as evidenced by a note in his diary on 8 January of that year: 'More archaeology in the study, throwing up the most surprising things, including a rather interesting 14-page essay from 1966, a justification for art, of which I haven't the faintest recollection.' The third piece, a short one on the function of literature, dates from 1 October 1966.

Because I do not know exactly what Parker intended to do with these three pieces at this point in *Hopdance*, yet the ideas in them are obviously important to an understanding of his aims in writing it, I have included them in this appendix rather than in the text of the novel itself.

I. Undated manuscript fragment, probably written in 1988:

The days of the world drawing in.

Many of us, perhaps most, sense the world ending in our time, or soon after. For how can the lure of idle weapons be forever resisted?

Meanwhile we have days to fill. Lives to conduct. Comportment to achieve.

II. Essay written on 17 May 1966 (words and phrases in bold are ones that Parker had drawn boxes or brackets around, either at the time of composition or after, and the pencilled epigraph was probably added later):

The care of posterity is greatest in them that have no posterity. BACON

May 17th, 1966

A total conviction that life as we understand it is moving towards annihilation. The annihilation will be physical, but that aspect of it will not matter too much, because it will be sudden and instantly overwhelming. What matters now is that, in our present situation, we are already dead. First question of everyone's life then is:

how should I respond to this predicament?

Most people will seek an anodyne, and the most popular anodyne will be to go on doing the things that people have always done, ever since this civilization, that is now in its dusk, dawned. One of these things is making art.

The people who were born to make art — as well as the usual quota of those who were not born for this purpose — are hard at it, as ever. For me, the most important fact to recognise about this activity is that it *is* an anodyne. To put it even more simply: writing poetry is escapist. The urge behind it is twofold: to communicate and to embody that communication in a permanent form. Because of the death of our civilization, communication through poetry on any meaningful plane is non-existent, the faculty of the vast majority of people to experience it having withered away. You can still communicate through poetry to your friends, of course, and a handful of other specialists, but this act in itself is an admittance of escapism. (It is, though, a very *dignified* form of escapism, and a very admirable one per se because of the difficulties involved in writing a poem.) As for poetry enshrining perceptions in permanent form, this is patently untrue for us: our culture, all of it, like many cultures before it, is going to be disappeared. Chaucer has lasted 500 years. Nothing written today has a hope of emulating *that*. We are in the act of putting the finishing touches to a tradition — a magnificent tradition — that is about to be extinguished for ever.

The artist who recognises this, and who is not satisfied with escapism, is in a tight spot. What to do? Give up writing? This is a very common reaction indeed, like the physical form of suicide. No other solution?

This depends on the way you feel about living in the death throes of a civilization. You may feel like going gaily berserk, and *celebrating* the fact that communication through art is a dead letter, as the Dadaists and Surrealists did, or, more recently, the Beats. This is a lot of fun, but of course it is, sadly, as escapist as writing neo-Augustan pastorals. It is a jolly romp, like wake games, and you are welcome to it if it satisfies you.

To return to the original question, which was: how do I respond to my predicament?

Enter Parker. For me, the most important response is the one which anybody facing any death has — to prepare yourself for the event. I am not quite sure what that *means* (and I don't think that even people with a profound belief in God's existence are sure), but I think I know what it *is*. It is a subjective reality, the most subjective of all. Shakespeare shows men preparing themselves to die, and then dying *correctly*, but he never attempts to define the nature of these events, because they are wholly internal and at the furthest point from human contact. There is only that superbly simple line of Edgar's — 'Ripeness is all.'

Art is an adjunct of life. Life is immeasurably more important than art. One reason why the attempt to make art does not seem to me to be a futile response to my predicament is that I can use it to achieve ripeness, to prepare myself for my own death, of course, but also to prepare myself for the larger death of which I am a tiny part. It is in this way that art is a religion, a meditation, a **communion** with yourself. Nobody seems to want it to be that, but I am dealing with facts here, not with ideals.

Can it be more than that? Yes, it can, (but not *much* more), because the fact is that, today, when communication through art, or anything else, is more difficult than it has ever been before, we *need* to talk to one another, desperately, like all sinking men. We need to get together.

There are several ways in which this is more possible than we care to believe. One of them is that the artist in his present predicament may consider himself absolved from the responsibility of perpetuating the tradition. Perpetuating the tradition was almost the major concern of the great writers of the last generation, especially Eliot, Yeats, Pound and Joyce... in theory. But in practice, by consummating the tradition, they removed the necessity for us, their descendants, to bear the responsibility of participating in it. Tradition, and the manipulation of it, depends entirely upon the existence of a sophisticated community. The shared habits, modes of thought, aspirations and preconceptions of a community are in fact what the tradition develops out of. We no longer live in such a community. The only people who are at all aware of the tradition are, at the one extreme, that handful of peasants in the remote parts of the country who are perpetuating the songs, epics, rituals and styles of life of their ancestors — if, indeed, there are any left who have not been made irretrievably self-conscious by the folk-lore collectors — and, at the other extreme, that handful of people who have taken a degree in English Literature. The former, the audience for whom Yeats longed to write, have their own artists and are centuries away from the vast majority of us in time. We can rob them, but we cannot give them anything. The latter make up the bulk of the audience for most contemporary literature. And even their relationship to the tradition is not a living one. The tradition for them is a diorama. For three or four years they look through the glass at it, and the tiny figures move, and the authoritative voice explains the significance and felicities and subtleties of the scene they are witnessing, but a diorama is not life, and they emerge into the real light of day. An extraordinary number of them – the overwhelming majority – never read contemporary poetry: partly because it is so uninteresting and so flaccid, but chiefly because they have been trained in the tradition, and that is something which has stopped: that is historical, they are not part of it, they are *observers* of it. Contemporary prose* is another consideration altogether. They do read contemporary novels – the ones that become fashionable. But when they do so, they do not feel, any more than most novelists do, that they are participating in a great tradition. They are specialists: the very idea[†] of specialisation prohibits even the possibility of a tradition.

It should be clear by now that the contemporary writer has no responsibility for the tradition, even if he wants it, which he should. His work must be done in a vacuum – that is always looked on as a depressing fact, but it has its advantages. It reduces the writer to a figure of less importance than he would care to be, but it also releases him from a great burden. He is free to create an autonomous art, as wholly twentieth-century as a synthetic fibre. He has no obligations to form or convention, or (and this is most important and least recognised) to genre. He should not waste time wondering whether he is creating poetry or verse or prose, a novel, a play, a short story, comedy, tragedy, or pastoral. These (at best arbitrary) terms have content only when a tradition is flourishing, when a poet is at once fulfilling his audience's expectations and taking advantage of those expectations. Milton could juggle the conventions of the pastoral elegy, or turn the epic conventions ingeniously to his own ends, as Spenser had done, in such a different way, one hundred years before him. Fielding could put paid to the form altogether, and yet revitalise it simultaneously, by writing his 'comic epic' of mundane life. Dickens could take this novel form and fuse into it the fulfilment of what his audience expected from its

---

* Parker actually wrote 'poetry', here, an obvious slip of the pen.

† As earlier in this paragraph, there is an obvious error in the manuscript here: 'they very idea.'

newspapers and its trashy drama, thus creating once again, maybe for the last time in England, a great popular form. This kind of activity, in which they all participated, is pointless for us, who have no audience expectations to fulfil or exploit. That is why almost all the literature being produced today by the universities, all the neo-Hardy or neo-Browning or neo-Augustan poetry, all the villanelles and sonnets and little square stanzas, all the George Eliot or Anthony Trollope or even Evelyn Waugh novels, seems so debilitated and has no effect on anyone at all, not even on the writers, who produce out of lack of something more exciting to do. These works are hollow; boneless freaks; they are not responding to the reality of their environment, and who can blame them, since that reality is so entirely dull — the kind of death we are enduring is not noble or exhilarating, of course, but it is also not alarming, it is Death, the frumpy middle-aged woman with her hair in curlers, drinking beer and watching the commercials on her colour television. Even neo-Georgian verse seems more exciting than that vision.

But to repeat the point: the writer today has neither a need for tradition nor a use for it. This has been recognised for about thirty years in a very popular dictum on contemporary poetry, one that every student of Eng. Lit. writes down on at least one exam in his time: the modern poet creates his own form — the content shapes the form. This dictum is wholly irrefutable, but it must be taken to its logical extreme — in modern art, the poet creates his genre, and, maybe, his audience. He begins his day with absolutely nothing. In one way, this is terrifying and oppressive, producing a sense of some crushing weight on the mind getting gradually heavier: in another way, it is breathtaking and heady, producing a sense of weightlessness and joy. These are the forces with which every modern artist has to contend.

To sum up so far: in the face of the death which is already rampant in our civilisation and of the annihilation that lies ahead, the artist stands a very big chance of being an escapist. One way in which his art can be meaningful is if he uses it as a means of cultivating his own soul in the face of destruction; and another is if he recognises it as inevitably an ephemeral and at the same time urgently necessary activity, one which he should have no illusions about. If he does look upon it in this way, then he can set about building his artefacts from scratch, bound only by the necessity to talk to people, to get in touch with them at the most effective level possible, owing nothing to the past and having no need to meet the demands of the conventions, forms, or even genres that his unimpressed generation has inherited.

The question now arises: *what* will the artist want to communicate, in the given situation? And the answer here is what it has always been, namely, his personal vision of things. Artists, like prophets, are born with a conviction that their way of seeing life and death is unique and valuable, and they have a compulsion to reveal it to other people. The reason why art is feasible is that everyone has this compulsion, at least everyone in his right mind, and everyone agrees that such a compulsion is an essential and indispensable part of reaching maturity and staying relatively sane once you're there. We have got to talk to each other about our condition. That is a sine qua non of our life. Without it, nothing. And that is the vital source of art, for the artist is simply a man with a more than average distinctiveness and persuasiveness and originality in his voice, one who can not only offer a worthwhile vision of his own, but can also help people to find the right words or perceptions or images or tones of voice to clarify and communicate their personal truths. That is his job now, just as it has always been, and, if anything, it is more important now than ever before, and less possible.

The only vision that I can imagine in our state is one involving a good deal of laughing. I carefully avoid saying 'comic' or 'humour', because these are terms from the tradition, they mean Chaucer or Mark Twain, Rabelais or Falstaff or Ogden Nash, and they are countered with 'tragic' or 'high seriousness'. The kind of laughing that we need to do today will not be contained by such definitions. And indeed, laughing never has been satisfactorily contained by any definition, thank god. Is Hamlet's laughter comic? Or humorous? Is Lear's Fool's? Those essays that have been written on the subject — Bergson's, Meredith's, Freud's, Pirandello's — are defeated by it, before they start. Defining a laugh is like trying to dole out slices of mercury, and the material wickedly glints and gleams at you as it slithers round the tray. This, for me, is one of its great characteristics. The laugh is the last stronghold of the stubborn human recalcitrance to be defined, the last stance taken by that Satanic mockery which lurks within every human personality, reducing all of man's libraries and museums and academies and pretensions and conceits to absurdity. In the very act of even thinking about it, I feel helpless and foolish. The laugh is the most complicated human response of all — is, to my mind, the only characteristically human response — and yet, or maybe therefore, it is one that our intellect will never even begin to annex.

The kind of laughing that Pinter elicits, or Ionesco, or Joseph Heller, is exceedingly profound and very enjoyable. To call it 'sick humour' or 'satire on life' or 'black comedy' is grossly inadequate, and an instance of how traditional terms will no longer work. It is a highly sophisticated and fundamentally human response to a vision of life which you recognise as peculiarly valid in our state of mortescence. It is a supra-verbal response (weeping is sub-verbal) — the complications of the laugh are so many, you could never reduce it to a series of words on a page. It seems to me to be that 'highest level of communication' possible in our time of which I spoke earlier, and it is the level for which I am striving.

Of course, what I am saying can be reduced to a banality such as 'let's all exit laughing', but that's not what I mean at all. There is no percentage in merely dying on a guffaw. The laughing that I am invoking is ultimately and probably unwittingly philosophical... though that statement is the most pompous one I have ever seen or heard of.

It is because of this vision that I ultimately feel that making art is not a futile response to my predicament. It is in the moments before death that those things which have seemed worthwhile in life become infinitely more precious than they have ever been before. We should enjoy those things to the utmost. Art can *help us to do that and can also help us* **to sustain the unspeakable pain of losing those things.** There is a very big audience indeed which still has the capacity for that enjoyment and that pain, and the artists are not fighting hard enough to take possession of it.

III. Essay written on 1 October 1966:

Oct. 1, '66

A function of literature is to liberate people from the prison of the character which they have created for themselves. Each man and woman creates a role for himself or herself to play; partly from the way in which people react to him, and partly from his own conception of his faults and virtues, he decides at a certain stage in his life that his character is *thus*, and thereafter proceeds to behave according to its dictates. This part which each of us casts ourself in is always a type-part, and we surrender to it because the alternative is to face the unbearable enigma within. In adolescence, we become aware of the incomprehensibility of our own nature for the first time, and we are confused and frightened by it. The search for an acceptable type-character in which we can subsume that incomprehensible mystery is a quest for survival. But it is completed by a kind of death. Because the character in which we imprison ourselves is a grotesque parody of our real nature: a reduction of our infinite potentialities to a miserable handful of traits.

As soon as we decide that those traits are what we are, we have closed the door to any really momentous influence. Thereafter, we will never admit that we may be wrong about something *basic*; we will never change an attitude to life that we have discovered to be distorting or malignant. Instead, we will behave in the way our created character is supposed to behave; we will behave predictably, and be relieved by our predictability right to the death, which may come soon if we have cast ourselves in the part of a criminal, or an alcoholic poet, or a reckless driver.

Literature should bring its reader to a crisis; he should confront his own invented character, and rebel against it. Poetry should destroy the deathly refuge of predictability, and plunge the reader into the exciting, ghastly open sea of his real nature. Poetry should transform the individual character from a state of become into a state of becoming. Great men are still becoming on their deathbed.